Making Wood Signs

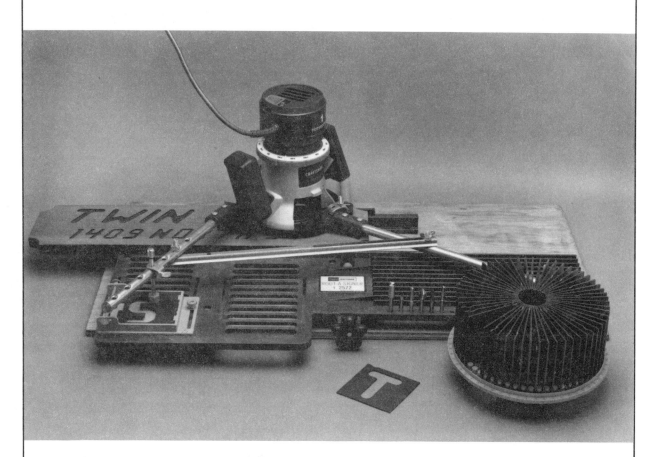

Patrick Spielman

 Sterling Publishing Co., Inc.　New York

Metric Equivalents

INCHES TO MILLIMETRES AND CENTIMETRES

MM—millimetres   CM—centimetres

Inches	MM	CM	Inches	CM	Inches	CM
1/8	3	0.3	9	22.9	30	76.2
1/4	6	0.6	10	25.4	31	78.7
3/8	10	1.0	11	27.9	32	81.3
1/2	13	1.3	12	30.5	33	83.8
5/8	16	1.6	13	33.0	34	86.4
3/4	19	1.9	14	35.6	35	88.9
7/8	22	2.2	15	38.1	36	91.4
1	25	2.5	16	40.6	37	94.0
1 1/4	32	3.2	17	43.2	38	96.5
1 1/2	38	3.8	18	45.7	39	99.1
1 3/4	44	4.4	19	48.3	40	101.6
2	51	5.1	20	50.8	41	104.1
2 1/2	64	6.4	21	53.3	42	106.7
2	76	7.6	22	55.9	43	109.2
3 1/2	89	8.9	23	58.4	44	111.8
4	102	10.2	24	61.0	45	114.3
4 1/2	114	11.4	25	63.5	46	116.8
5	127	12.7	26	66.0	47	119.4
6	152	15.2	27	68.6	48	121.9
7	178	17.8	28	71.1	49	124.5
8	203	20.3	29	73.7	50	127.0

Special Edition Sears 925-129
Printed July 1995
© 1992 by Patrick Spielman
Published by Sterling Publishing Company, Inc.
387 Park Avenue South, New York, NY 10016
Manufactured in the United States of America

Contents

Safety Information 4
Introduction 5
1 Woods for Sign-Making 9
2 Designing Wood Signs 16
3 Basic Tools and Machines 34
4 Cutout Letters 39
5 Hand-Carved Signs 59
6 Routed Signs 70
7 Sign Routing and Carving Machines 96
8 Making Large Signs 102
9 Making a Huge Sign 115
10 Sandblasting Signs 119
11 Finishing Signs 132
12 Guidelines for Starting a Wood-Sign Business 141
13 Keeping Your Tools Sharp 144
14 Patterns and Design Ideas 148
   Color Section Photo Credits
   Index 191
   Color section opposite page 64 192

Below is a list of recommended accessories that will help you make beautiful signs using power tools. These accessories are available in the Sears *Power and Hand Tool Catalog* and at most retail stores.

Model No.	Description	Page No.
25176	Sign Layout Kit	45, 96
25196	Sign Layout Kit	99
2573	Letter Template Kit	93
25187	Deluxe Pantograph	98, 99
25172	Foot Pedal	101, 144
26003	Rotary Pantograph	97
25126	Rout-A-Copier	100, 145
2572	Rout-A-Signer	99
25921	Drill Press Stand	145
6672	Drill Bit Sharpener	145
6491	Ginding Wheel Dressing Stick	146
6660	Router Bit Sharpener	146
21645	Tool Grinding and Sharpening Handbook	146

Safety Information

It is essential that anyone using power and hand tools follows several safety guidelines. They are as follows:

1. Always consider the safest way to perform the job.

2. Read the instruction sheet and follow the safety rules as outlined by the manufacturer of your tools.

3. Remember that in most cases accessories will make the power tool safer to use. One example is the use of a router pantograph with a router.

4. Use goggles, ear plugs, respirators or whatever else is necessary to protect yourself.

5. A sharp tool is a safe tool. Carefully read Chapter 13, "Keeping Your Tools Sharp," for the proper ways to sharpen your tools.

Introduction

Signs abound all around us. They direct, locate, restrict, inform, identify, motivate, and sometimes aggravate our daily lives. Signs give us good and bad messages of all sorts. Flickering neon, lighted plastic, and rusting metal signs obscure and cheapen commercial areas across the country. Conversely, wood signs blend in with all environments and offer a desirable change of pace (Illus. I-1).

The continuing popularity of authentic, well-crafted wood signs is very real, and the reasons are manifold. Perhaps the major reason is that wood itself has a quality of uniqueness and individuality that stands eloquently alone—enduring and "honest." This very quality has led many plastic and metal sign companies to imitate the appearance of wood with artificial graining and texturing. This is not design integrity, and we all know it. Authentic wood signs do not give a deceptive impression. Whatever the message of an authentic wood sign, we subconsciously assume that it is said sincerely and honestly. Remember, a sign is your "front door." It gives others their very first impression of your home, business, farm, or community.

Wood signs have many other advantages over their offensive plastic and neon counterparts. Wood signs truly blend in with trees, foliage, shrubbery, stone, or water. Beautiful country landscapes and architecture can be least disturbed by unobtrusive, well-executed wood signs. Yet, they delicately and effectively attract the eye because they are each unique. Wood signs maintain their desired natural appearance for a long time, much longer than other kinds of signs which eventually fade, blister, crack, rust, or literally fall apart. When assembled and finished properly, wood signs become more beautiful with age. Regardless of what most people think, wood signs best endure the turbulent natural elements of moisture, sun's rays, snow, sleet, and ice. They also best resist vandalism. As wood signs get older, they impart an impression of endurance, long establishment, and permanence (Illus. I-2).

Wood signs can be easily fabricated to take advantage of three-dimensional design. Letters, numbers, and decorations can be (1) cut into the surface, (2) raised from the backing, or (3) a combination of both (Illus. I-3).

This book is heavily illustrated with sample signs in many shapes, styles, and sizes. These will be very helpful to you whether you are a novice or an accomplished producer of wood signs.

Becoming skilled at wood sign work is easy. One can start small and work up to larger or more involved signs, with each new one offering a differ-

Illus. I-1. A park preserving the giant redwoods. Note how the unobtrusive sign blends in with the surroundings.

Illus. I-2. Wood signs endure and actually become more beautiful with time. (Designed and crafted by Pudge DeGraff.)

Illus. I-3. Effective combination of cutout letters (attached) with engraved (cut-in) letters and design logo makes a very attractive sign. (Designer and fabricator unknown.)

Illus. I-4. A sign simply executed with individual letters sawn out and attached to produce a raised letter effect.

ent challenge. There are essentially two distinct areas of proficiency that one should continually strive to improve upon and eventually master. These are (1) design and (2) execution of basic woodworking skills. Making quality wood signs requires an intimate marriage of graphic design and technical woodworking. Many books are available devoted to each subject. This book, for the most part, will not deal with or repeat this type of information. However, in the following pages you will be guided, step-by-step, through each area of wood sign work. Each new sign will improve your expertise, and before long you will have people knocking on your door requesting your skills.

At this point you may want to turn sign-making into a business enterprise. You can start small with a minimum of equipment—with just the bare necessities of a knife and chisel you can learn to carve eloquent wood signs (Illus. I-2). With a coping saw or a portable sabre saw you can cut out letters of any size and style (Illus. I-4). This book offers little advice on sign business management. However, it must be pointed out that a good business potential does exist. Why? Everyone loves wood and almost everyone needs some sort of signage. Think about it for a moment! Developers of residential areas and home owners want entrance signs, name signs, and street signs (Illus. I-5). Business and professional people want impressive, distinctive signs. City, county, and other public agencies need signs to identify and direct people to roads, parks, recreational areas, and public buildings. Profes-

Illus. I-5. This example of wooden street signage in a Florida development is both unique and attractive. (Designer and fabricator unknown.)

sionals who make small routed name signs freehand or by machine, when set up in shopping centers, fairs, and tourist areas, can earn extra money.

This book will show you how to produce different kinds of popular wood signs. One chapter deals with basic hand-carved signs (Illus. I-6).

Another chapter deals with cutout or sawn letters. Several chapters are devoted to routed signs (Illus. I-7 and I-8), as these are currently the most popular and offer the greatest speed and variety of sign-making. Also included is a chapter covering sandblasting. Throughout the book are tips, shortcuts, and advice offered on subjects of design, material selection, tools and machines, finishing, and related project ideas. The last chapter supplies a wide variety of letter and alphabet patterns.

Unless otherwise indicated, the signs illustrated as examples in this book have been fabricated by the author.

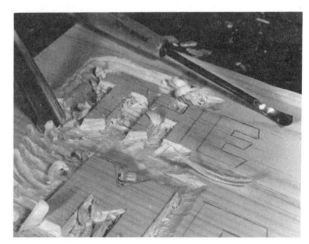

Illus. I-6. Hand-carved wood signs require a minimum of tools, but more effort than other kinds of wood signs.

Illus. I-7. Freehand routing produces small signs quickly, as shown by this single-stroke work.

7

Illus I-8. Another example of an incised routed sign—just one among endless possibilities.

Woods for Sign-Making

The selection of wood materials for sign-making should be based upon the following requirements:

(1) Service (interior or exterior). Will the sign be exposed to humidity, sun's rays, weather, etc.?

(2) Desired appearance (overall design effect). Do you want the sign to look smooth and modern, or rough and rustic?

(3) Workability. Sawn-out letter work does not require wood with easy cutting properties as do hand and router sign carving.

(4) Freedom from defects. Will cracks, knots, or warpage detract from the sign's appearance or interfere with cutting operations?

(5) Cost. Do not skimp. A better grade, although more expensive, will eliminate much aggravation.

(6) Availability. Can you always get it quickly and easily (locally), or must it be shipped to you?

Woods for Interior Signs

Woods for interior signs have only one important criterion. They must be properly dried. Almost any species or kind of wood material can be used as long as it gives you the desired appearance and is dried to a moisture content appropriate for interior use. All fine furniture hardwoods can be used for indoor signs. Kiln-dried mahogany, walnut, butternut, cherry, etc., are ideal for hand-carved or router-carved signs. Softwoods such as pine, redwood, basswood, and cedar are very desirable for all kinds of work.

Woods for Exterior Signs

Woods for exterior signs do not need to be kiln-dried, but they must not be green either. A moisture content of 12 to 15 percent is a very satisfactory range for most parts of the country. This level can be achieved by proper air drying of fresh-cut boards or lumber (Illus. 1-1). Redwood is one of the best overall choices, but its major disadvantage lies in its high cost. Western red cedar, northern white cedar, and cypress are more economical. They have similar positive properties in their resistance to the deteriorating effects of decay and weathering. However, redwood is generally regarded as far superior in its easy working properties. Any type of wood can be used for exterior signs if it is kept dry. However, most signs are usually exposed to the sun's rays and moisture. During weathering, some species of wood may degrade more rapidly than others. Brief descriptions of various woods and their suitability for exterior signs follow:

Basswood is soft and lightweight. The heartwood is pale yellowish brown with occasional

Illus. 1-1. A supply of 2-inch white cedar for exterior signs is piled and stickered for air drying.

darker streaks. Its sapwood is creamy-white or pale brown. Basswood does not, as a rule, have attractive graining, and it is usually painted or stained with opaque finishes. It has a fine, even texture and straight grain that makes it easy to work, especially for hand-carved signs. Basswood does not have exceptional weathering qualities, so it must be carefully finished. Basswood grows in the eastern half of the United States. Most of it comes from the Great Lakes, Mid-Atlantic, and Central states.

Cypress grows commercially in the Southern states. The color varies widely. Its sapwood is narrow and nearly white. The heartwood ranges from light yellowish brown to dark brownish red, brown, or chocolate. It is moderately hard and one of our most decay-resistant woods, making it especially useful for sign posts. As a rule, it is not the easiest wood to carve by hand or with the router.

Douglas fir essentially comes from the Northwestern Coastal and Rocky Mountain states. It has rapid growth, as often characterized by its graining and spacing of growth rings. The difference in hardness between its spring and summer growth often makes it difficult to router-carve cleanly and smoothly. It does not weather well, with a high tendency to check and distort in hot and dry environments. Douglas fir is fairly economical. Rough-sawn Douglas fir (lumber and plywood) does make attractive signs, but it must be properly finished for exterior use.

Pine comes in many different types. White pine, ponderosa pine, and sugar pine rank high in dimensional stability with little shrinkage or distortion. Clear, knot-free pieces are ideal for hand and router carving, with sugar pine being the best. Lower grades can be used for rustic signs. Southern yellow pines are inexpensive but do not have the good overall qualities for carving and routing of the other pines. The pines will weather well if properly finished and kept away from soil and excessive moisture.

Spruce is very similar in appearance and color to pine, but the varieties from the Southern states have more difficult working properties. It is essentially a construction material, as is Douglas fir. It is economical and readily available at most lumberyards and building centers. Eastern spruce is light in color with little difference between its heartwood and sapwood. It is easily dried, lightweight, easily worked, and has moderate shrinkage. Its appearance makes it suitable for interior sandblasted signs.

Cedar is of two major types: white and red. The cedars are among the best overall choices for exterior sign work. They are economical, have high resistance to decay, can be worked easily, and weather well. The cedars are generally straight-grained and have uniform texture. They sandblast well and are easily carved by hand or router. They are lightweight, moderately soft, and easily dried.

The red cedars grow in the Eastern forests and some limited areas of the South Atlantic and Gulf Coastal plains. A similar species, western red cedar, grows primarily in the Pacific Northwest. The heartwood of red cedar is reddish brown to dull brown, and the sapwood is nearly white.

White cedar grows in the Atlantic states and eastern part of the United States. The greatest sources are probably in Maine and in the Great Lakes states. The heartwood of white cedar is very light brown, and the sapwood is nearly white. It is lightweight and shrinks very little in drying. It is easily worked, highly resistant to decay, and holds finishes exceptionally well. White cedar can be router-cut cleanly, and some of it sandblasts well, depending on how it is cut from the tree.

Redwood (Illus. 1-2) grows principally in California, but it is available nationwide. The sapwood is nearly white. It is very easy to work because of its straight and uniform grain. Redwood shrinks or swells very little and is highly resistant to decay. In short, redwood is a good choice for any kind of

Illus. 1-2. Redwood has a uniform texture and other excellent qualities for hand-carving, routing (shown), and sandblasting.

wood sign work. It is the easiest of any wood to sandblast. Its only disadvantage is its comparatively high cost for clear and select grades. However, because of its overall superior qualities, it is usually worth the extra expense. Sometimes the costs can be offset by purchasing a lower grade, such as "construction." Often, small, clear pieces can be cut out between knots and glued together again to make large clear pieces. Redwood and cypress are the only two woods that are naturally resistant to termites.

Pressure-Treated Wood

Pressure-treated wood is available to the home craftsman at lumberyards and building centers. In this special wood, preservatives are forced deeply into cellular fibres with large vacuum-pressure treating systems. The preservatives prevent wood-destroying organisms from getting to their food source, thereby protecting the wood from decay and rot. The treating process results in wood with a soft green color that needs no further finishing. However, pressure-treated wood is stainable or it can be painted any color. Pressure-treated wood is available in several wood species with southern pine being very widely used. It is generally heavier than comparable untreated wood because it is saturated with preservatives. Pressure-treated wood

is highly recommended for posts in contact with soil and moisture.

It is possible to give regular non-treated posts a brush-on or dip treatment of preservative yourself, but the long-term protection is not nearly as great as with pressure-treated wood. The service life of dry, treated pine in contact with the soil is two to five years. A brush-on application will add one to three more years. A dip treatment gives $\frac{1}{10}$- to $\frac{1}{8}$-inch penetration and will give an added service life of five to ten years. Pressure treatment lasts a lifetime.

Selecting and Buying Lumber

Selecting and buying lumber for wood signs, as for any worthwhile woodworking project, should be done carefully. Check to see what kinds of materials are available locally. As mentioned before, signs for outdoor use do not need to be made from kiln-dried wood, but the wood should be dried to the point where it is in equilibrium with the moisture in the surrounding atmosphere. In northern Wisconsin, for example, fresh-cut lumber is available for direct purchase from small sawmills. It must be stacked outside and allowed to dry from six months to a year before use. (Illus. 1-1). Signboards can be 1 or 2 inches thick, with the latter preferred for two-sided and larger signs.

In northern Wisconsin, signs with rough-sawn surfaces are seemingly more popular than those made of smooth-surfaced stock. Rough-sawn stock can be purchased directly from sawmills, and rough-sawn western cedar and redwood are often available at lumberyards. It is possible to give a smooth board a rough-sawn textured surface yourself. Simply pull it rearwards obliquely along the blade as shown in Illus. 1-3. It can also be done on the table saw. However, in this case you feed the stock as usual along the rip fence. Use an old blade with a tooth set out a greater distance than the rest. This tooth will "chew up" the surface, giving it a rough-sawn appearance.

It is suggested that rough-sawn boards be touch-sanded lightly (Illus. 1-4). This light sanding highlights the texture and removes protruding slivers and fibres that make layout and routing difficult.

Obviously your design should be worked out before you select and prepare your stock. Thus, you

Illus. 1-3. Giving a smooth board a rough-sawn texture. Here the surface is pulled lightly backwards along a band-saw blade.

Illus. 1-4. Rough-sawn boards are lightly touch-sanded to highlight the texture and, at the same time, remove problem slivers or protruding fibres.

can position patterns to avoid knots or other defects before cutting the sign blank to final size and shape.

Remember that when purchasing smooth-surfaced boards from lumberyards, they are finished to less than their nominal (name) or rough-sawn size. For example, you know that when you buy a "two-by-four," it actually measures 1½ inches by 3½ inches. A 6-inch board is 5½ inches wide, an 8-inch board is 7¼ inches, a 10-inch board is 9¼ inches, and a 12-inch plank is actually 11¼ inches.

Lumber Grain Patterns

Boards and planks are cut from the log in different ways—usually with "vertical" or "flat" grained

faces (Illus. 1-5). You will find that in most species of wood the boards with flat grain tend to cup and warp a lot more readily than boards with vertical grain. Some species may be more difficult to router-cut or sandblast on vertical grain than flat grain. This is especially true with Douglas fir and some cedars.

It is also important to remember that vertical-grain boards are more dimensionally stable than flat-cut boards of the same wood. In other words, vertical-grained boards do not shrink or swell in size across their width as much as flat-grained boards do. This is an important consideration if the signboards are to be encased or circled by a wooden frame. Allowance should be made for wood expansion when putting frames around signs of solid wood.

VERTICAL GRAIN   FLAT GRAIN

Illus. 1-5. The difference between vertical- and flat-grain wood. Boards with vertical grain are more dimensionally stable and tend to warp much less than boards with flat grain.

Hand-Hewn Signs

Hand-hewn signs (Illus. 1-6) and posts (Illus. 1-7) are very popular, as these represent an era of the far-distant past. Hand-hewn planks can be effectively simulated by texturing the surfaces with various edge tools as shown in Illus. 1-8—1-10.

Rustic Slab Signs

Rustic slab signs of all sorts can be made with a little imagination. Slabs from sawmill edgings, or

Illus. 1-6. This routed sign with the hand-hewn effect is easy to make.

Illus. 1-7. Surfaces of big timber posts can be worked with the adze to produce a hewn appearance.

Illus. 1-9. Using an inshave to "chew up" the edge. Make some cuts against, as well as with, the grain.

Illus. 1-8. Make cross-grain cuts randomly with a hatchet.

Illus. 1-10. The surface is worked in the same manner. Hatchets, chisels, and adzes can also be used, but the inshave produces the best routing surface.

Illus. 1-11. This slab from a sawmill would have little value as lumber but makes a good rustic sign.

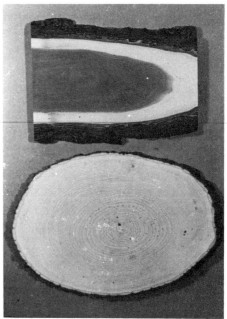

Illus. 1-12 (above left). A slab cut diagonally from a tree creates a very natural look. Illus. 1-13 (above right). Slabs cut in different directions have different shapes.

slabs you simply cut yourself with a chain saw, make effective and unusual signs, as shown in Illus. 1-11 and 1-12. Slabs can also be treated with polyethylene glycol to keep the bark on (refer to the book *Working Green Wood with PEG*, also published by Sterling). Small slabs of this type (Illus. 1-13) are also easily accessible at art and craft shops. They are also available by mail order.

Plywoods and Other Sheet Materials

Plywoods and other sheet materials are often

required for certain, usually larger signs. Exterior plywoods with rough-sawn surfaces are available, particularly in fir, cedar, and redwood. Smooth, exterior fir plywood has little aesthetic value in sign work. It is primarily used as a backing that is either not visible in the structure or completely painted to opaque its wild grain. Even when carefully painted, the grains often eventually "telegraph" through the finish, which is objectionable in the eyes of some people. A new sheet material especially designed for smooth, painted surfaces is available. This is a plywood with a resin-coated-paper-overlaid surface (Illus. 1-14). This material is ideal for making inexpensive cutout letters that will be painted and attached to another sign backing. Plywoods are obviously not suited to hand-carving and sandblasting. However, they do deserve consideration for router-carved signs (Illus. 1-15). The glue lines will dull ordinary high-speed steel router bits quickly. Carbide bits will not dull nearly as quickly, so use them when routing plywoods and other hardwoods.

Illus. 1-14 (above). Some common sign-making materials include rough-sawn planks (cedar), smooth 1- and 2-inch boards (redwood), and plywood overlaid with resin-coated paper. Illus. 1-15 (right). This large routed sign with an irregular profile shape is best made of plywood. Note the rough-sawn texture. It was spray-painted black and then touch-sanded to highlight the saw marks.

2

Designing Wood Signs

A properly executed sign is one that is expertly crafted from a good design. Many people believe that good design depends upon artistic talents. Obviously, possessing these qualities would be helpful. However, if you are not a "natural" or you are untrained in graphic artistry, don't be discouraged. This chapter will assist you to the point where you can create well-defined, artistic wood signs quickly and easily (Illus. 2-1–2-3).

Give careful attention and critical study to all of the signs you see daily. Soon you will notice that some have that special appeal while others do not. Try to distinguish just what it is that makes one sign more appealing than another. Is it the choice of letter style, the appropriate size and spacing, the color, or the arrangement and combination of individual elements? Study the signs illustrated throughout the pages of this book. Many are of rustic motif, yet appear to be carefully planned and executed. Others are designed to fit into more modern and contemporary surroundings (Illus. 2-4).

Use your own imagination, but also select desirable features from signs that appeal to you. With an awareness of all kinds of signs you will soon establish your own priorities and individual stan-

Illus. 2-1. Small name signs are good "starters."

Illus. 2-2 (above left). Large, bold, block letters are easy to read. Illus. 2-3 (above right). A very basic sign. Note how the rounded corners and pegs help to make the sign interesting.

Illus. 2-4. A "woodsy" look is emphasized in this modern sandblasted sign. (Designed and fabricated by Sign Classics, Inc.)

dards of good design and taste. You will become capable and confident when judging sign design qualities.

Your first and primary concern may be originality. Do not worry about this. Copy and use the alphabets and plaque designs provided through-out this book. Each sign will be your creation because it will have its own wording, as well as individual symbols, logos, or appropriate decorations to complement the lettering or overall effect.

Essentially, design in sign work involves delivering the appropriate graphic message by attracting the viewer's attention in a positive manner. The overall appearance should do everything possible to enhance the function of the sign. A very ornate and overly decorative sign, for example, may defeat the primary functions of clarity and easy readability.

You should make a careful analysis of your design to be sure that the sign actually does what it is intended to do. For example, is the lettering legible or would another lettering style be easier to read? Script and Old English letters are more difficult to read than most other alphabets. Avoid using complex, decorative typefaces on signs that require maximum legibility. On the other hand, the extremes of "balloon fat" or heavy bold letters do not read as easily as letters of medium line-thickness or stroke-width. When selecting an alphabet with a decorative face, be very cautious— the letter design should convey the appropriate feeling and meaning. See Illus. 2-5.

Other questions in analyzing sign designs include: Is too much design crammed into the space? Would more background space improve the overall appearance? Are words and phrases

Illus. 2-5. This decorative lettering is certainly appropriate for a Mexican restaurant. These two different type styles are effectively used, providing emphasis and contrast. And even though the letters and lines are close together, the message is still easy to read.

laid out so they can be read with a sensible meaning? (Be careful when separating words or phrases into different lines. The words in each line must read clearly and be meaningful together.) Does the sign have sufficient contrast to be legible?

The proper use of color is an effective way to achieve contrast. Backgrounds should be of a contrasting color to that of the letters and designs. Remember that light-colored letters against a dark background appear larger than the same-size letters painted dark against a light background. Contrast or emphasis can also be achieved by using different-size letters to draw the eye to the key word or phrase of the message. Avoid using too many different type styles on the same sign, however. Trying to create some variety and interest may be a good idea, but combinations of several letter styles are more likely to create an element of confusion than a feeling of consistency and unity.

Observe, with an analytical eye, all forms of graphic artwork. Look at newspaper and magazine ads, and run through the Yellow Pages. You will quickly notice the sharp, eye-catching designs incorporated into the logos and identifying artwork of the large companies and progressive small businesses. You may notice also that many current graphic artists and advertising illustrators use similar techniques. For example, they tend to space letters very closely together, much more closely now than was the accepted practice a few years back. Letters often touch each other, as do words and lines of words—some even overlapping. This technique gives the designer the opportunity to use large letters in otherwise tight areas.

Letter Size

The first technical consideration is to establish the desirable size (height) of the individual letters. Be conscious of the fact that signs are located at various distances from the viewer. Letters that may appear to be very large sitting on your workbench diminish rapidly in size as they are positioned progressively farther away. Consequently, determine the maximum required distance from which the sign must be easily read. Certain styles of letters are more legible than others. Bold, fat, simple block letters are the easiest to read—especially if the viewer is travelling by in a motor vehicle. The travelling speed of the viewer, his/her visual acuity, color contrast, and the presence of distracting surroundings are some of the variables that make strict rules for letter sizes difficult to establish. However, the following chart may be helpful as a guide to determine the optimum letter sizes for people with 20/20 vision.

Distance (in feet)	Letter Sizes (height in inches)
100	1¾ to 2
200	3½
400	7
600	10½
800	14
1,000	17½
1,300	22 to 25

Often you will have designed your letters to be a certain specific height for optimum visibility. However, as you work out the design you find that the letters do not fit horizontally in the space available. The option then is either to reduce the size of the letters or condense them. See Illus. 2-6.

One quick way of determining the proportional horizontal space that will be required for letters enlarged to a specific height is to use the diagonal line method. For example, if you wanted to enlarge a letter (as printed in this book) to a height of six inches, draw a horizontal line six inches above and parallel to the base line. Then draw a diagonal line through the letter (or through an imaginary

Illus. 2-6. The problem, shown at the top, is that the desired letter height does not fit the horizontal space. The solution is either (left) to reduce the size or (right) to condense the letter width to fit the space.

rectangular space surrounding the letter) until it intersects the top horizontal line. Complete the rectangle as shown in Illus. 2-7.

Once the preferred letter height is determined, and assuming total space is no problem, enlarge the sign letters to this size. Be sure to arrange or allow for appropriate spacing between letters (and words) so the "art" is easily readable. One key point is to eliminate unnecessary wording. Discourage the inclusion of too much information.

Letters can be enlarged in several ways. The first, and easiest, way is to use an office copier machine to enlarge (or reduce) the letters. They can also be enlarged with the same graph-square or grid system commonly used by woodworkers to enlarge their project patterns. Inclined letters can be created by enlarging the original on a slanted grid, and the grid system can be used to make condensed or expanded letters from the original pattern. See Illus. 2-8 and 2-9.

Full-size patterns custom-developed for your

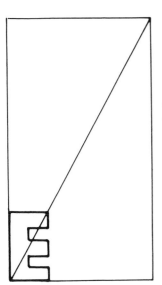

Illus. 2-7. The diagonal line method quickly determines height-to-width ratio for enlarging letters.

signs can also be ordered by mail. Precise letter designs, symbols, and borders for any sign from one inch to 100 feet in height can be obtained in full size from companies specializing in this service. They use graphic art computers and special programs. All you do is send in the general specifications, including the overall size, the copy, the letter style, art for symbols or logos, and the general layout with preferred letter heights. This information is fed into a computer and you get a full-size print (pattern) by return mail. It will have the letters expanded or condensed (as necessary), aligned, and spaced perfectly while maintaining the original design concept.

Full-size enlarged letter patterns in various typefaces and sizes can be purchased at retail stores. They are available in the form of full-size printed plans or as die-cut letters (templates) in plastic, wood, and cardboard (Illus. 2-11).

Letter Spacing

Letter spacing is an important design consideration. Letters should not be crowded too closely together or have unequal gaps. The letter *A*, for example, fits more closely next to *T* than *E* or *M*. Once the word is composed and laid out full size, step back the maximum distance and view it critically. Have others look at it and get their opinions. Does the sign have character? Is it clean and crisp? Is there continuity in style? Does it convey satisfactorily the intended theme or feeling? A good, well-spaced, properly aligned, and consistently styled letter arrangement will work for you. Make your layout on paper first, so changes can be made as necessary until you achieve your standard of perfection. (Note: Be sure, at this point, as well as immediately before carving, to have the sign's originator check it for accuracy.)

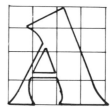

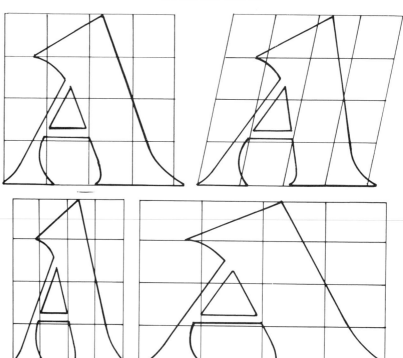

Illus. 2-8. Enlarging by the grid or graph-square method. The original is above. At right is a straight enlargement. At far right is an enlargement with a design modification using a slanted grid.

Illus. 2-9. The graph-square method can be modified by using rectangular grids to (left) enlarge and condense or (right) enlarge and expand the original example in Illus. 2-8.

Illus. 2-10. Full-size alphabets are available in print from companies that provide full-size paper patterns for woodworking projects. Also shown are full-size pre-cut plywood templates that can be homemade or purchased pre-machined.

Arranging the Words

Determine which geometric profile shape is most appropriate for the sign. There are three basic choices: (1) rectangular-horizontal, (2) square or round, or (3) rectangular-vertical (Illus. 2-11). Almost all signs will fit into one of the above categories. The selection of the most suitable overall sign profile from the above three may be dictated by requirements such as: (1) the width and height of the area in which the sign will eventually be hung or placed, and (2) the type of signpost that may already exist. Study Illus. 2-12—2-20. Often you may have to "play" with trial-and-error layouts, using scaled pencil sketches on graph paper to match the optimum letter size and the desired arrangement and order of words. The object is to fit everything satisfactorily onto a sign blank of the

Illus. 2-11. Arrange the words to complement the different geometric shapes.

Illus. 2-12. Size can be used to give emphasis to important words.

Illus. 2-13. Each of these three signs is interesting in itself through the use of different letter sizes.

Illus. 2-14. A vertical layout. Note the clarity achieved with the different styles and sizes of letters.

Illus. 2-15. Individual, pre-cut, full-size letter patterns, such as these of cardboard, make "trial-and-error" layout easy.

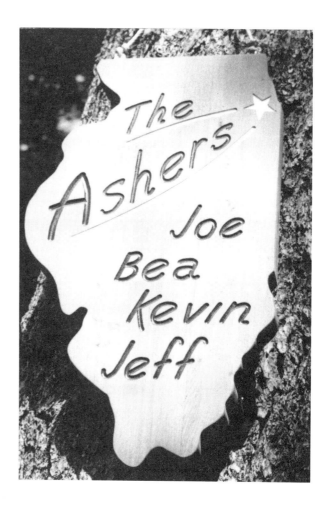

Illus. 2-16 (right). The size and shape of the sign determine the layout.

Illus. 2-17. A perfectly square sign with logo and wording centered.

Illus. 2-18. Another (basically) square sign, but here the layout is not symmetrical.

Illus. 2-19. Extending the vertical "legs" on some letters adds an element of height to the layout without increasing width.

Illus. 2-20. A curved layout can be an interesting arrangement that reduces length as well.

desired overall shape. When confronting this sort of problem, be sure to give consideration to the overall shape of the total sign before finalizing the height of the letters. Very often the letters will have to be reduced or enlarged slightly more than expected to fill up excess blank space or avoid crowding.

Amateurs and beginners wanting to make their enlarged layouts quickly and easily will find the use of enlarging projectors more suitable than the graph-square method for their design work. The two basic kinds of projectors are *opaque* and *overhead*.

Opaque Projectors

Opaque projectors create an enlarged image of any non-transparent object. Printed pages, photographs, and drawings in black-and-white or color can be enlarged easily. Opaque projectors range in price from very inexpensive to very expensive. They all work best in a darkened room.

Overhead Projectors

Overhead projectors (Illus. 2-21) project bright,

Illus. 2-21. An overhead projector can be used to enlarge images in a lighted room.

enlarged images in a lighted room. They will enlarge to any size from a 10-inch-square transparency (transparent acetate, clear plastic, or glass) that lies flat on the face or stage of the projector. The overhead projector is, as a rule, less expensive than a good opaque projector. The image is always clearly reproduced. Overhead projectors are more convenient, more portable, and more versatile.

While overhead projectors can be fairly expensive items to purchase, they can often be rented or borrowed. They are available through camera or audio-visual equipment supply stores. Schools widely use overhead projectors.

Preparing Art for Projection

Enlargement begins by using the same lettering aids technical artists use, known as dry-transfer or rub-on letters. These consist of pre-printed lettering on pressure-sensitive sheets as shown in Illus. 2-22. They are easy to use. Simply transfer the letters to another surface by burnishing (rubbing) over the letter on the carrier sheet as shown in Illus. 2-23. Wide selections of typefaces, borders, designs, and symbols are available. Dry-transfer supplies are relatively inexpensive and can be purchased at office supply stores, artist-craft shops, or directly by mail order.

The dry-transfer letters are transferred to a sheet of clear plastic film or even directly onto a piece of window glass. This layout is then placed on the projector table and an enlargement of any size can be made by moving the projector towards or away from the projecting surface (a wall will do). Once the desired size is achieved, the enlarged image is traced (Illus. 2-24). It can be traced onto paper (for a permanent copy) or directly onto the wood sign blank. One good method is to make a paper copy and then refine the traced lines and the work and space arrangement before transferring the design to the wood. The paper patterns are retained and the copies make useful sales tools.

Sooner or later someone will want you to reproduce a specific design from a printed business letterhead, sales brochure, or newspaper ad. Designs of this type can be enlarged in one of two ways: (1) draw squares over it and enlarge it freehand by the graph-square or grid method, or (2) have a transparency made of it which is subsequently enlarged on the overhead projector. A

Illus. 2-22. Pressure-sensitive lettering can be selected from catalogues. Shown is 180-point type (1¾ inches high)—about the largest available.

Illus. 2-23. To apply dry-transfer letters for the preparation of original artwork, first rub them with a dull pencil, ballpoint pen, or similar blunt instrument. Then, lift the sheet carefully.

Illus. 2-24. Here, individual letters are traced from an enlarged projected alphabet.

transparency of any printed art can be made for you by anyone who owns a thermo-copier transparency-making machine. Most schools have this equipment, as do major business offices and some public libraries. It only takes a few seconds to have a transparency made. The 3-M Thermo-Fax® copier-transparency maker is a good machine to use. Use the 3-M transparency film 8½ × 10½ inches type 558, which produces a black image on a clear background (Illus. 2-25–2-27). Many of the new office copy machines also have the capability of making transparencies from original line art.

Once you have gone through the processes of using press-on letters, overhead projection enlargement, and making transparencies, you will see how very simple copying, enlarging, and designing really is. This experience will be your most valuable design asset. Any conceivable design or pattern can be copied and enlarged for your own creative sign work (Illus. 2-28). Soon you will be clipping magazine ads, leafing through children's

Illus. 2-25. Complete alphabets can be transferred to transparency sheets and subsequently enlarged to any size desired.

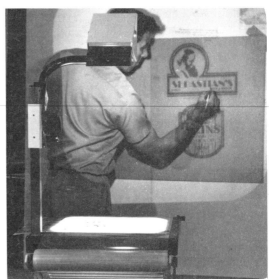

Illus. 2-26 (above left). A transparency film can be made from a newspaper advertisement. Illus. 2-27 (above right). The enlarged ad, projected from transparency film by an overhead projector, can then be traced.

Illus. 2-28. The finished sign in wood. This one was made by sandblasting.

coloring books, and digging into similar resources. Before long you will have a file of designs that can be combined with various alphabets to make truly superb custom-designed signs.

Once you get into sign-making, commercial jobs will begin to come your way. Often the client will supply his own design, or will be financially able to hire a commercial graphic artist to design his sign. Some will approach you and provide you with the full-size layout. Then all you have to do is transfer it to the wood and carve, rout, or blast the design, in or out as preferred.

Transferring the Pattern to the Wood

Transferring the pattern to the wood is a simple task, as shown in Illus. 2-29 and 2-30. Illus. 2-29 shows a paper sign pattern being traced and transferred to the wood with carbon paper. Illus. 2-30 shows the use of a "pounce wheel." Before removing patterns, be sure that all lines have been transferred. On rough-sawn surfaces use carbon paper *and* a pounce wheel because it is difficult to see clearly all the tooth markings of the pounce wheel on these surfaces. When transferring pat-

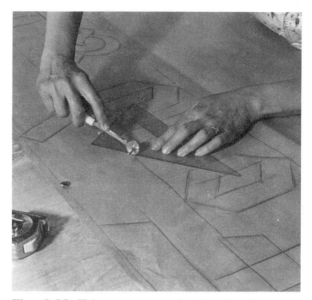

Illus. 2-30. Using a pounce wheel makes the transferral of large patterns quick and easy.

terns to smooth-surfaced wood with a pounce wheel, the carbon paper can be eliminated.

After the letter patterns are outlined on the wood, silhouette them with chalk (Illus. 2-31) or soft-tip markers. This is especially helpful when doing freehand router carving so you know which side of the line to cut on and which areas need to be removed or left uncut.

Computer-Assisted Designs

Illus. 2-32—2-35 show examples of computer-assisted designs for different signs. Illus. 2-36—2-41 show different design options for one sign.

Illus. 2-29. Transferring the enlarged pattern to the wood with carbon paper.

Illus. 2-31. The layout can be chalked in to make it easier to see during routing.

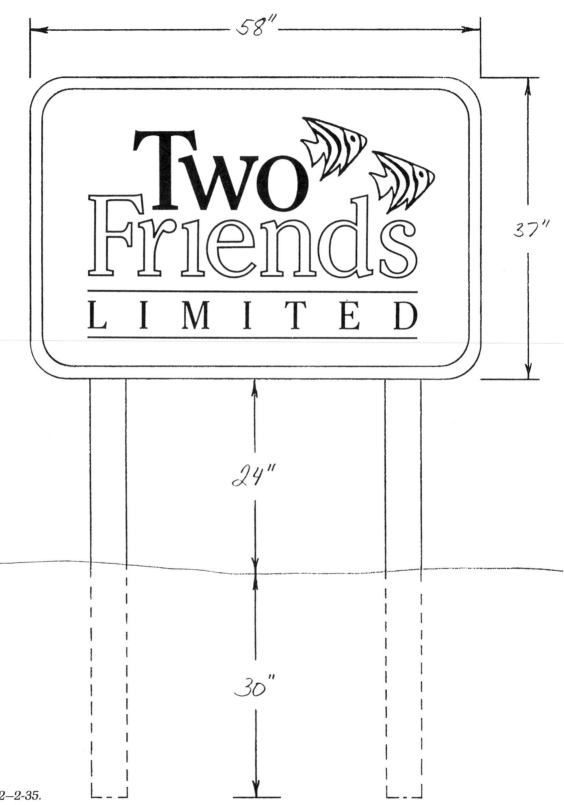

Illus. 2-32—2-35.
Examples of computer-
assisted design work.

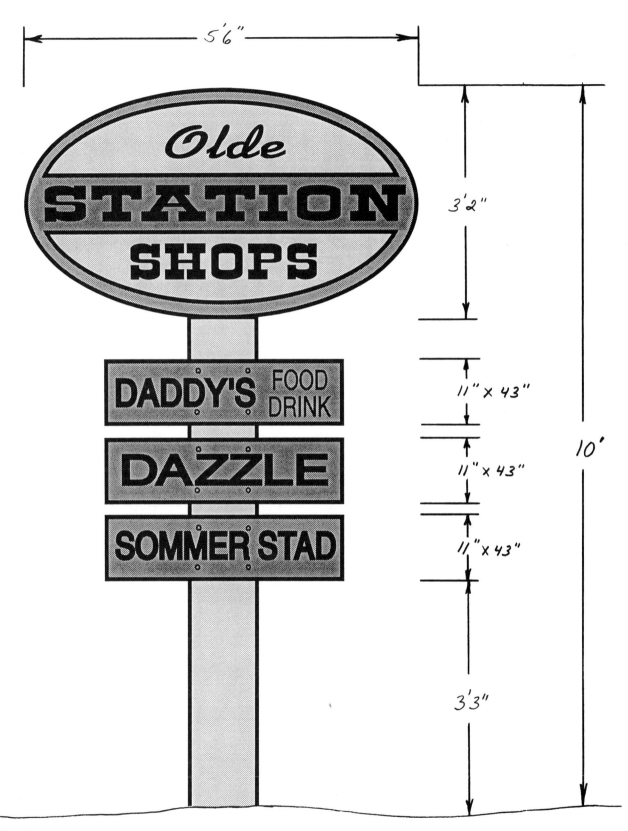

Illus. 2-33.

Illus. 2-34.

Illus. 2-35.

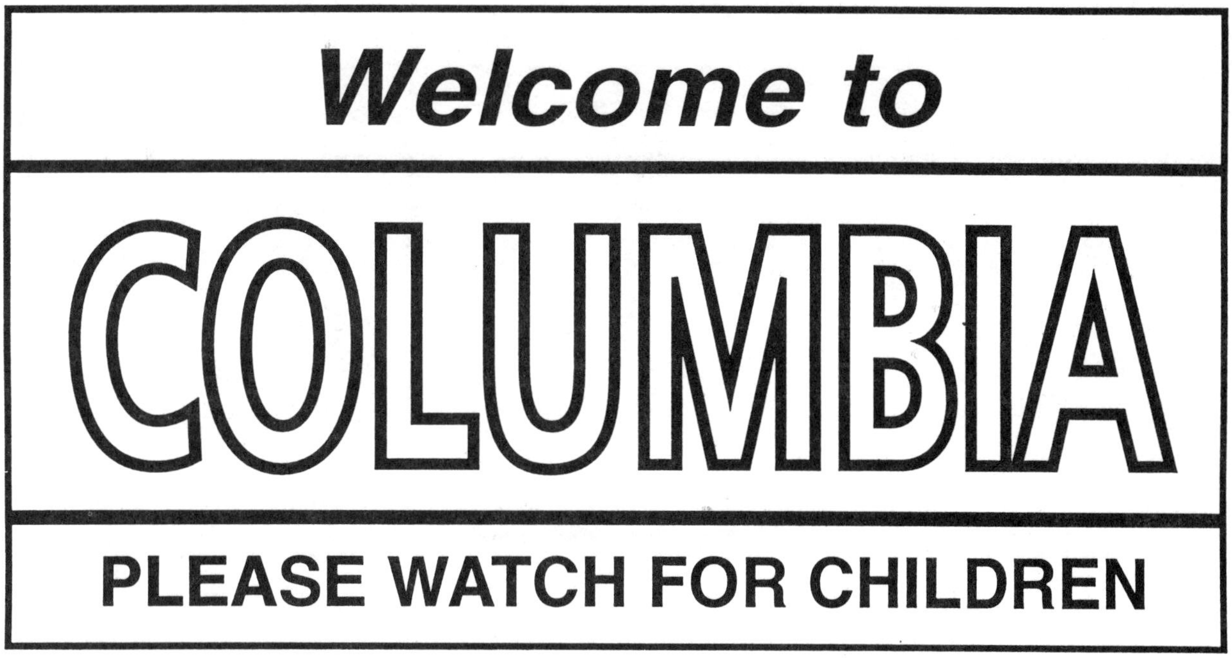

Welcome to
COLUMBIA
PLEASE WATCH FOR CHILDREN

Illus. 2-36—2-41. Examples of computer-assisted design options for one sign. (Drawings courtesy of Spielmans Cedar Works.)

WELCOME TO
COLUMBIA
Please watch for children

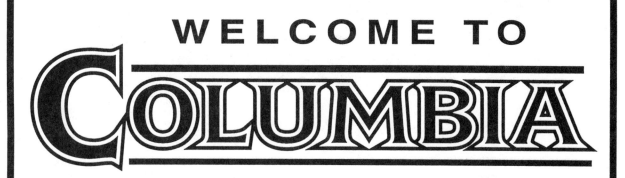

Illus. 2-37.

Illus. 2-38.

Illus. 2-39.

Illus. 2-40.

Illus. 2-41.

3

Basic Tools and Machines

You will need the usual array of small household hand tools, including tape or bench rules, straightedges, squares, hammers, and screwdrivers. Here, let's take a brief look at some of the additional tools and machines that are basic to most wood sign fabricators. This chapter will omit the usual "how-to" operating and safety instructions because this information is probably redundant for most of you and is very adequately presented in many other books devoted to wood crafts. (Check at your local library.) However, particular instructions that apply specifically to the craft of making wood signs will be presented later in other chapters, such as those devoted to carving, sawing, routing, and sandblasting. If you do not own or have access to the tools or power equipment, check with the rental services that may be found in most cities. If you are just beginning you may

Illus. 3-1—3-3. A table saw (above) makes crosscuts and rip cuts quickly and accurately. Slow but effective, this inexpensive coping saw (top right) can be used for sign work requiring irregular and curved cuts. A portable electric sabre saw (bottom right) is a good multi-purpose tool.

also consider jobbing out some of the work to local professionals, such as carpenters, cabinetmakers, or other woodworkers.

Saws

Any good handsaw or portable circular saw, suitable for straight-line ripping and crosscutting, is a must item for sizing your material. The table saw (Illus. 3-1) makes both crosscuts and ripping cuts quickly and accurately. For making cuts that are irregular or curved, you can use a simple coping saw (Illus. 3-2), a portable electric sabre saw (Illus. 3-3), a scroll saw (Illus. 3-4), or a band saw (Illus. 3-5).

Planing Tools

Planing tools are often necessary for smoothing the surfaces and edges of sawn boards. Planes are used to prepare boards for gluing into wider or thicker sizes. Unless planing tools are available, it is necessary to always purchase material that is already planed to your specified finished size. Various kinds of hand planes (Illus. 3-6) are available. Portable power planes are also available, but they are expensive and have little advantage over well-sharpened, properly adjusted hand planes. Serious woodworkers like to use the jointer (Illus. 3-7) for trueing the edges and surfaces of boards. A thickness planer is a luxury piece of equipment unless you are a full-time professional wood-

Illus. 3-4 (above left). The scroll saw is ideal for making cutout letters and similar inside or outside curved cuts. Illus. 3-5 (above right). The band saw makes easy work of both straight and irregular cuts in thin or thick materials.

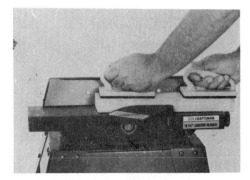

Illus. 3-6 (above left). Planing the edge of a board with a jack plane in preparation for gluing. Illus. 3-7 (above right). A small jointer can do big planing jobs.

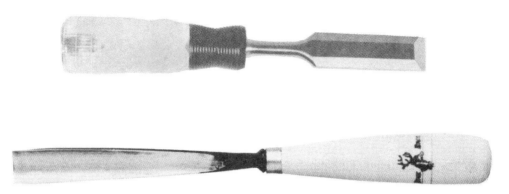

Illus. 3-8 and 3-9. Chisels (top) and gouges (bottom) are inexpensive yet necessary tools for making hand-carved signs.

worker or sign-maker. This machine reduces boards to uniform parallel thickness.

Shaping Tools and Routers

Shaping tools and routers are required if a sign is to be given an interesting shape or formed edge, with an overall professional look to it. A lot of sign work can be done by a skilled craftsman using simple, ordinary chisels and gouges (Illus. 3-8 and 3-9). Various wood files or rasps are helpful in making hand-carved signs. A simple jackknife or utility knife is very useful in the hands of a skilled "sign mechanic."

The portable electric router (Illus. 3-10) is a whole shop in itself because of the wide range of bits and attachments that are available. Routers come in many sizes, styles, and with various standard or optional features. Some makers of routed signs prefer a very small, lightweight, high-rpm tool for working redwood and for edge-forming work. Others, like myself, prefer a heavy, high-powered unit for making deeper and wider cuts in tougher woods. Features that are worth considering when purchasing a router for sign work include: weight, rpm, horsepower, type of on-off switch, lighted work area, vacuum attachment, collet size (bit capacity), and the availability of parts and repair service.

Having a router that will carry bits larger than the usual ¼-inch-shank diameter affords the craftsman the opportunity to purchase and use bits available for large production, industrial routing machines.

Router Bits

The old saying "You get what you pay for" is espe-

Illus. 3-10. A router is one of the most important tools for the serious sign-maker. Many different features are available to satisfy individual needs and preferences.

cially true here. Inexpensive bits are good for a few jobs. They can be resharpened when dull, but the problem is that they dull quickly. Good-quality, high-speed steel bits hold up very well when routing softwoods such as redwood. However, the cedars (particularly the white cedars) dull even the best high-speed steel bits rather quickly. Good carbide bits are probably more economical and they will give you less grief and frustration in the long run. Note, there is good carbide and cheap carbide as well. When shopping for carbide-tipped bits, look for thick carbide. Some bits are tipped with carbide that is too thin, and after one or two

sharpenings the carbide becomes dangerously thin and the bit must be thrown away. Remember that carbide requires special grinding wheels. It is strongly recommended that all of your bits be sent out to professional resharpening services. Bits must not only have proper clearance angles, but they must be properly balanced as well; otherwise, their ultra-high-speed vibrations are both dangerous and difficult to handle skillfully.

Drilling or Boring Holes

The drilling or boring of holes is often necessary for one job or another. This class of work can be done using the old bit and brace, the portable electric drill, or the drill press machine. An adjustable expansive bit (Illus. 3-12) is useful for making large holes of any size. If you own a small portable electric hand drill (with only a ¼-inch chuck), consider buying a set of spade bits (Illus. 3-13); they will allow you to drill holes up to 1 inch in diameter with your small drill.

Dowel Jigs

Dowel jigs are available in several different styles.

A good one is often a tremendous help to the serious sign-maker. It is especially helpful when gluing boards edge to edge to make large sign blanks. Dowels in this case are used more for the purpose of aligning the pieces during gluing rather than imparting additional joint strength. If glued properly, edge-to-edge joints are stronger than the wood itself.

Clamps

Clamps are needed when gluing and assembling larger signs. Bar clamps (Illus. 3-14) (or clamp head fittings for pipe) are necessary when gluing boards together edge to edge. Handscrew clamps (Illus. 3-15) or "C" clamps are used to hold work steady for carving and routing by clamping it to benches. They are also used to apply pressure when gluing pieces of wood face to face to make a thicker piece.

Sanders

Here again, individual preferences will vary. Pad or vibrating sanders (Illus. 3-16) are nice for fine finishing work. Belt sanders are more powerful and cut faster.

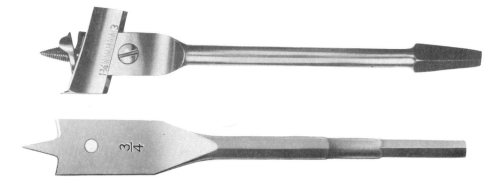

Illus. 3-12 (top). This expansive bit is adjustable for large holes of any size. Illus. 3-13 (bottom). Spade bits like this, used to make holes up to 1 inch in diameter, are available to fit ¼-inch electric drills.

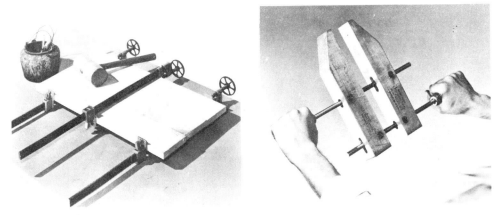

Illus. 3-14 (above left). Boards glued edge to edge with bar clamps. Illus. 3-15 (above right). Handscrew clamps have many uses.

Illus. 3-16. A pad sander can be used for finish work. Note the dust-collecting attachment.

$$\boxed{4}$$

Cutout Letters

There really isn't anything especially difficult about making cutout letters (Illus. 4-1). Any fairly imaginative and reasonably proficient woodworker can enlarge and saw out individual letters, compose them into words, and attach them to some sort of panel backing—creating a fabulous, dimensionally interesting sign. This chapter will provide some ideas for such signs and offer a few tips to make this class of sign work even easier.

Background Sign Panels

Using plywood panels for sign backing makes the job especially easy. Very large wood signs can be made stronger, faster, and more economically with plywood backings than with any of the other wood sign systems described in this book. Several kinds of exterior-grade sheet plywoods are available with interestingly textured surfaces. Check with your building materials supplier and you will probably find plain, rough-sawn fir, cedar, and redwood in textured, grooved (Illus. 4-2), reverse board and batten, and other suitable designs. They all make excellent backgrounds for cutout raised letters. The sign in Illus. 4-3 was laid out with the Sears Wood Sign Layout Kit, Model 25176, which can be purchased through the *Power and Hand Tool Catalogue.* The knots in the cedar en-

Illus. 4-1. Different materials and finishes give different effects. Counterclockwise from top left: letters run together in edge-laminated woods; veneer-faced plywood; solid rough-sawn cedar; solid finished pine.

Illus. 4-2. The grooved plywood backing shown here allows for quick assembly of the sign backing. (Designed and fabricated by Charles Kinsey.)

Illus. 4-3. Knotty cedar cutout letters are mounted to a redwood backup. This interesting sign is ideal for outdoor use because of the material used.

hance the appearance of this sign. By using carbon paper furnished with the kit, you can lay out letters and numbers rapidly and accurately. The kit is inexpensive and comes with two styles of letters, Old English and Block. Templates are 6, 8, and 10 inches high.

Plywood Cutout Letters

Plywood cutout letters (Illus. 4-4) have several advantages over letters cut from solid wood. They do not crack or warp, and they can be made in very large sizes (height and width) without gluing. For letters and decorations that will be painted with opaque, pigmented finishes, any exterior sheet materials can be used. There is available a resin-coated-kraft-paper-overlaid plywood which is ideal for smooth, uniform surfaces that are to be painted. One serious disadvantage of plywood is that it seldom is available in sizes thicker than ¾ inch. Consequently, to achieve anything thicker two or more pieces must be glued together face to face. If good glues are used and the letters well-sealed and finished, they will endure the exterior elements as long or longer than plastic-formed letters.

Solid-Wood Cutout Letters

Making cutout letters of solid wood requires

40

Illus. 4-4. Solid weathered wood, diagonally planked, makes an attractive background for the painted cutout plywood lettering of this sign, seen along a Florida highway. (Designer and fabricator unknown.)

some precautions—especially if the letters are to be exposed to the weather. Most letters look better if they are cut from the wood with the grain running vertically on the face of the letter. Select letter styles that are "fatter," with few thin or narrow areas. Regardless, most letters will have areas of "short grain." An example of short grain is shown in Illus. 4-5. These areas are the weakest parts of the letters, and cracks or separations might develop during drastic changes in humidity and temperature. Plywood letters obviously do not have

this problem, because the veneer plies are assembled with alternating grain directions. However, the cut edges of plywood may be unattractive to some people, particularly if transparent stains are selected for finishing. Conversely, thicker solid-wood letters have a more authentic, rustic look. They also are more adaptable for making clean, router-cut edges.

The short-grain cracking tendencies can be minimized by gluing a thin piece of exterior plywood to the back side of the letter blank (Illus. 4-6) before sawing out the letter. Use any good exterior, waterproof glue. The thin, exposed plywood edges are hardly noticeable.

The usual steps involved to cut out thick solid-wood letters are demonstrated in Illus. 4-7—4-10. Super-large letters (those 24 inches high or greater) are made principally the same way. I believe larger letters require progressively thicker stock—whatever is available and economically practical. Thick and wide planks will usually require lamination (gluing narrow planks edge to edge to increase the width of stock, as in Illus. 4-11). In some extreme cases, it may also be desirable to increase thickness by gluing boards together face to face or using ¾-inch-thick plywood as a backing glued to the rear of the letters (Illus. 4-12).

It is a recommended procedure, when laminating, to rip planks wider than 6 inches in half and then glue the pieces back together. This step relieves internal stresses that might induce future

Illus. 4-5. This beautiful thick letter of solid wood may crack at the area of "short grain" pointed out here.

Illus. 4-6 (above left). Thin plywood glued to the back of a solid wood letter prevents cracking in "short grain" areas and adds extra thickness to the overall letter. Illus. 4-7 (above right). When possible, crosscut all letters to equal length (height) before transferring the pattern to the wood.

Illus. 4-8 (above left). Some curves are more easily and uniformly cut by boring than sawing. Illus. 4-9 (above right). Jigsawing on the inside opening of a very thick letter. Here the guide and holding attachments of the jigsaw were removed to afford a thicker-than-usual cutting capacity.

Illus. 4-10. Band-sawing is the choice method for all outside cuts on thick stock.

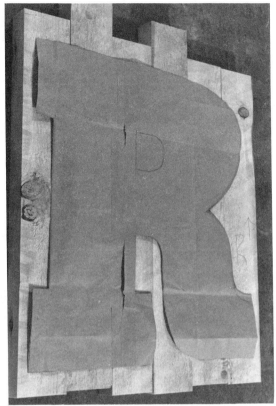

Illus. 4-11 and 4-12. Super-large letters (these are all 24 inches high) must be made by gluing pieces together edge to edge. The completed letters, above, were made by gluing narrow pieces of 2-inch stock edge to edge. They were backed with ¼-inch exterior fir plywood. Note the router-cut edges.

warping. Try to obtain planks that have vertical grain rather than flat grain. Vertical grain does not shrink and swell as much, and tends to warp less. Remember, routing the edges gives a neat, finished look. Be sure to finish all exposed surfaces of outdoor letters, including the backs.

Mounting Letters

Whenever possible, attach the letters to the sign backing panel with screws or lag bolts driven in from the rear (Illus. 4-13). Driving fasteners through the faces of letters should only be done as a last resort. However, there are times when rear mounting is impossible—such as on double-faced signs and when letters are attached to storefronts. In cases like this, there are a few options:

(1) Glue the letters on with waterproof silicone mastics. This is fast, easy, and generally permanent. Indoor sign letters can be "pasted" to the walls with panelling mastic (adhesive) or hot-melt glues.

(2) Use non-corrosive finish nails and exterior glue. If the letters and backing are previously finished, you will not get the maximum holding power of the glue. Also, if you assemble before

Illus. 4-13. These house numbers were glued and screwed (from the rear) to this ¼-inch pre-finished plywood backing, which was then nailed to the house.

finishing, the subsequent painting and staining around the letters will be time-consuming and aggravating.

(3) Use metal fasteners only, going right through the faces of the letters. Countersink the screw or bolt heads. Then plug or fill the holes and finish to match.

Standoff Letters

Standoff letters are attached the same way (usually with method 3 above), but with some sort of

Illus. 4-14. A stylish application of cutout, shaped, standoff wood lettering. (Designer unknown.)

Illus. 4-15. Vertically connected house numbers make an interesting departure from the conventional individual numbers that read horizontally.

Illus. 4-16. After a name has been sawn to its normal profile shape on a board of parallel thickness, an unusual name sign can be created by making one diagonal bevel cut.

unobtrusive spacing material between the letters and the sign back panel. Standoff, cutout letters give the sign yet an extra dimension of depth. This method casts interesting shadows (Illus. 4-14) and also makes future staining or painting around the letters much easier than when the letters are mounted directly to the panel. Spacers can be small pieces of wood or other non-corrosive material.

There are several low-cost layout kits available. Sears has two such kits for laying out letters from 2 inches up to 10 inches. Illus. 4-17 and 7-10 show these kits.

Illus. 4-17. The Sears 25176 Wood Sign Kit. The templates are 6, 8, and 10 inches high and are in Old English and Block style. This product is helpful in making signs of cutout letters using a sabre saw, band saw, or router.

Cutout Letter Designs

Crafting individual letters (Illus. 4-18) or designs and attaching them to a flat panel is perhaps the easiest way to create a dimension of depth in wood signs. A lot can be done with a minimum of tools and equipment. The attractive, contemporary sign shown in Illus. 4-19 was made using only an electric sabre saw (or coping saw). The letters and ornaments were cut from exterior plywood.

Using a router, you can round over (Illus. 4-20 and 4-21) or cove-cut the edges of letters that have been cut from solid wood. This adds more interest and professionalism. The faces of cutout letters can also be decorated by router carving or sandblasting.

The idea of decorating or working the faces of letters can be carried even further. Some very distinctive letters can be made by hand-carving and sculpting the faces. One company still specializing today in handcrafted, ornamental, carved wood letters is Spanjer Brothers, Inc., of Chicago. This company has been in existence, hand-carving letters and wood decor, since 1896. The fact that they have enjoyed continuous business all these years attests to the public's long-standing acceptance and demand for handcrafted woodwork in sig-

Illus. 4-18 (above left). Some examples of cutout letters. Illus. 4-19 (above right). This attractive sign, designed and fabricated by Don Zinngrabe, was made with just a few basic tools.

Illus. 4-20. Rounding over the edges of scroll-sawn letters. The use of this special router pad allows these letters to be routed without clamping.

Illus. 4-21. This special shop-made router base with a minimal clearance opening around the bit is ideal for edge-routing small letters and designs. The router will not tip with this base, as is likely to happen when standard bases with larger openings are used.

Illus. 4-22. An example of the fine work done at Spanjer Brothers, Inc.

nage. With the current trend towards "real" wood, coupled with the present popularity of historical restorations, their business is going strong. Span-

jer Brothers supplies solid wood-sculpted letters in all sizes (Illus. 4-22) to other sign companies that do not have the capability to craft their own.

Illus. 4-23 and 4-24 show a good alphabet pattern for band-sawing letters.

Victorian Signs

A charming sign displaying your house numbers (Illus. 4-26) and/or a sign just to say Welcome (Illus. 4-26) provide a final note for the Victorian home design. Illus. 4-27 and 4-28 are two patterns for signs that can be hung or mounted against a wall. These are just two of a wide assortment of

Illus. 4-23 and 4-24 (opposite page and page 48). An alphabet pattern for band-sawing. All the inside openings are cut away by sawing directly inward from the outside.

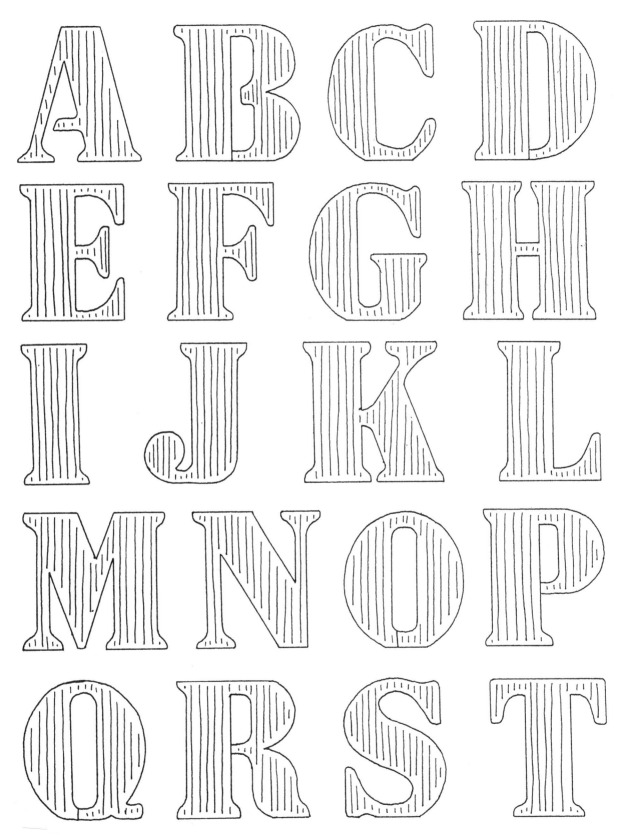

Illus. 4-23.

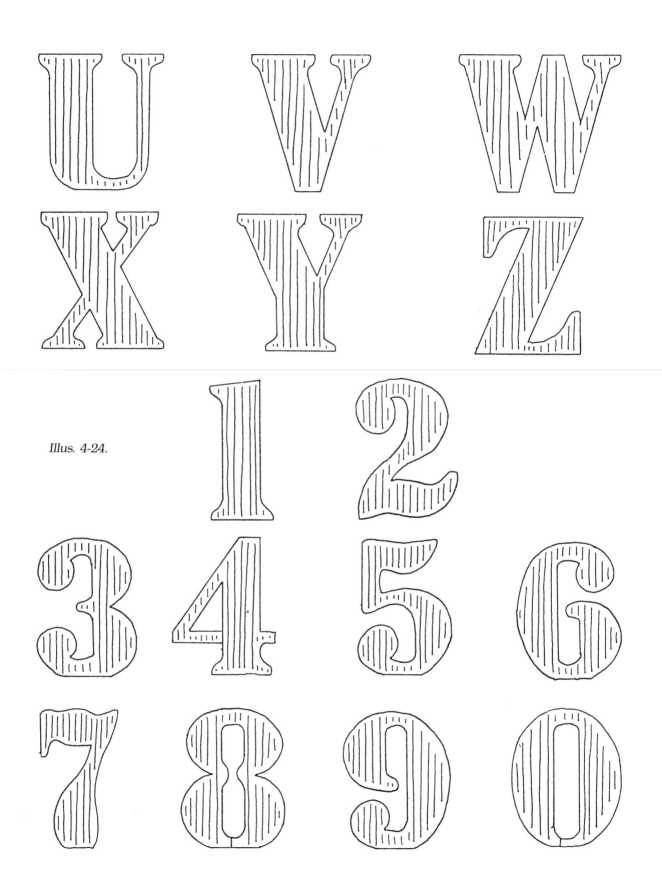

Illus. 4-24.

patterns that it is possible to use. Illus. 4-29—4-31 are patterns for an entire easy-to-read ornate alphabet and numbers to be used on Victorian signs.

Sharp curves and outlines of a very small radius can now be cut easily with the new scroll-cutting band saws and constant-tension scroll saws. This allows the craftsman to make beautiful wood signs of ornate letters and distinctive backing boards. Raised wood letters, border scrolls, turnings, and optional carving features can be combined to make some very distinctive and attractive Victorian signs.

You can make a raised border easily by sawing it from separate stock and then attaching it to the sign-board backer. The border stock for the sign-board patterns shown in Illus. 4-28 and 4-29 should be about ¼-inch thick. If for some reason you enlarge these patterns more than suggested, then make the border thicknesses proportionally thicker. If your sign-backer board is cut from plywood, then you can use ¼-inch exterior plywood for border material and for the numbers or letters, as the case may be. If using solid wood for the sign board, use solid wood or plywood ¼ inch thick to cut the letters/numbers and border piece(s).

Note: When making borders, letters, and number to be mounted to backer boards made from solid wood, be sure to align the grain of *all* pieces and segments so that it runs in the same direction. Since all solid wood expands and shrinks with changes in humidity, each component of the

Illus. 4-25. This house-number sign has ¼-inch-thick raised letters and borders.

Illus. 4-26. This welcome sign features raised lettering and border designs with decorative turnings and ornate plugs carved from dowels that conceal mounting fasteners (if used) at each corner.

Illus. 4-27. Full-size half-pattern sign board suitable for house numbers or other messages.

℄

50

Illus. 4-28. Half-size half pattern for the welcome sign border and border detail.

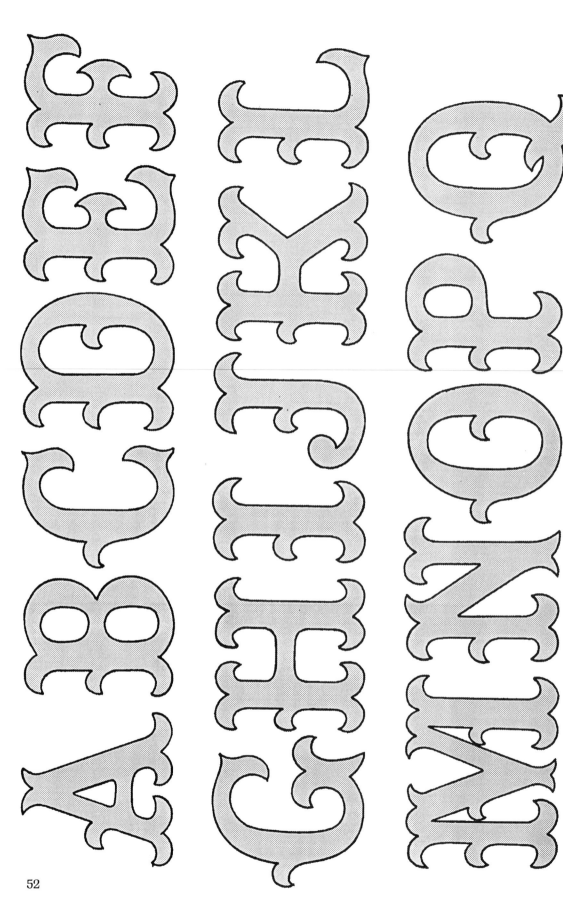

52

Illus. 4-29. An ornamental Victorian alphabet with matching number designs (Illus. 4-31). Enlarge the alphabets and numbers 140 percent if using them with the enlarged sign blank shown in Illus. 4-28.

Illus. 4-31.

sign will move together, thereby minimizing serious cracks and checking.

There are two ways to cut out the border. First, you can cut it in segments of two or four layers all at one time (Illus. 4-32). The total pieces of the same shape that are needed are determined by whether the sign will be a single- or double-faced sign. The border segments can be butted end to end as necessary (Illus. 4-33). Actually, stack-sawing is a great advantage, saving time and material. Both halves (or all four quarter-segments) of the border pieces will have cut shapes that are identical.

The border piece can also be sawn from one thin board pre-sawn to the same overall outside size and shape as the sign-backer board (Illus. 4-34). It's easiest to cut the outside profile of the sign-backer board and the outside shape of the border stock when the two pieces are stacked together and cut out at the same time.

Glue and tack the border pieces down using waterproof adhesive and short brads (½ inch by No. 20). Tack sparingly; you simply went to hold the stock tight against the backer board until the glue sets. You can also clamp or tape down the border if you don't want to use nails (Illus. 4-35).

The welcome-sign pattern calls for four decorative round corner plugs. They are just short lengths (about ⅝ inch) of ¾-inch-diameter dowel stock with pre-carved ends. These plugs also conceal flat screws if the sign is being mounted to a wall. Otherwise, they are intended to be decorative only.

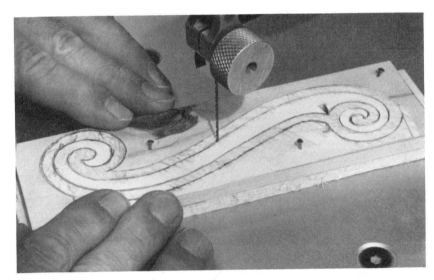

Illus. 4-32. A technique for making raised borders. Here two layers of border scrolls are cut at one time by stacking them together.

Illus. 4-33. The border scrolls are butted together, and then glued and tacked to the sign blank. The two vertical pieces are made with the "short grain," so they will expand or contract with any movement of the thicker sign-board backer.

Illus. 4-34. Scroll-sawing a one-piece border from ¼-inch-thick pine.

Illus. 4-35. Letters and/or numbers are sawn from solid lumber, with the grain running in the same direction as the sign board and attached with waterproof glue and brads.

Victorian Sign Post

The Victorian sign post shown in Illus. 4-36 is intended to carry a sign blank 20 inches in width. The arm can be extended or shortened to accommodate other sizes of sign board patterns if desired. The hanging sign board shown in Illus. 4-36 can be used with it. It was sawn from 1½-inch-thick cedar decking material glued edge to edge. The post detail is shown in Illus. 4-37 and 4-38.

Normally, the vertical post member should not be shorter than 8 feet, nor longer than 10 feet in overall length. This allows adequate material for the in-ground installation. Cut the horizontal arm to 25½ inches overall to accommodate a sign that's 20 inches in overall length (width). Dado the arm

Illus. 4-36. Victorian sign post and sign. Many other bracket designs could also be used. The sign board is 20 inches in overall length.

into the vertical post to a depth of approximately 1¼ inches. This cut or recess begins at a point 12 inches downwards from the top plate. The plate (under the turned finial) is simply a 1½-inch-thick plank cut 4½ inches square with ½-inch-radius rounded-over edges. Simply nail it into the end of the post.

Use a ⅜ × 6-inch lag bolt to attach the horizontal arm to the vertical post. Drive it into the end of the 4 × 4-arm. However, note from Illus. 4-37 that a length of 1-inch-diameter dowel is pre-set vertically into the arm near its attached end. This provides a secure anchor for the lag bolt, making a very strong right-angle joint.

The bracket (Illus. 4-38) is essentially decorative in purpose. It can be from ¾ to 1½ inches in overall thickness and glued in place if so desired. If you are pre-painting it, simply tack it on with corrosion-proof finishing nails set below the surface, and fill the holes.

Finally, your house numbers can be attached vertically to the sign post if desired. Simply enlarge the individual number patterns shown in Illus. 4-30 or 4-31 so that each number measures approximately 3½ inches in height. Cut the numbers from solid wood or plywood. Paint a contrasting color and attach them with silicone cement, finish nails, or screws.

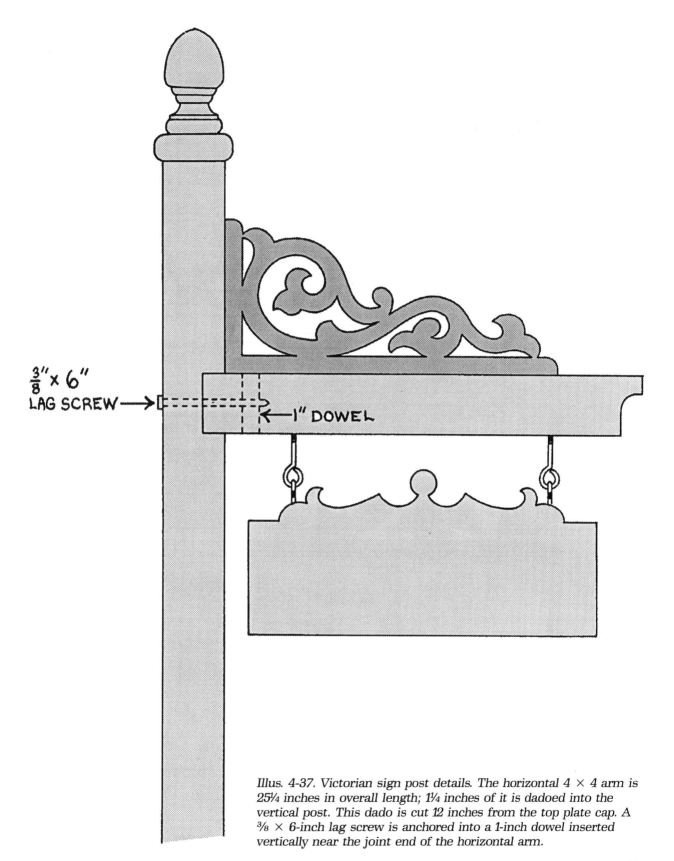

$\frac{3}{8}'' \times 6''$
LAG SCREW →

← 1" DOWEL

Illus. 4-37. Victorian sign post details. The horizontal 4 × 4 arm is 25¼ inches in overall length; 1¼ inches of it is dadoed into the vertical post. This dado is cut 12 inches from the top plate cap. A ⅜ × 6-inch lag screw is anchored into a 1-inch dowel inserted vertically near the joint end of the horizontal arm.

Illus. 4-38. The bracket pattern for the Victorian sign post. Enlarge it to approximately 20 inches in overall length.

$\boxed{5}$

____ Hand-Carved Signs ____

Making hand-carved signs demands more patience and artistic skills than any other form of sign work. However, the extra efforts invested afford the craftsman a far greater reward in pride and personal satisfaction. The range of proficiency in the craft/art will depend upon your technique, ability, and persistence in becoming a wood-carver. As with any form of woodworking, every project (sign) you carve will give you additional experiences that can be helpful and applied to the next piece of work.

Hand-carved wood signs can be separated into two basic categories: (1) *incised carvings* (making incisions) in which the letters (or characters) are cut into the surface, and (2) *raised or relief* work, in which the background surrounding the letters or design is cut away. Signs may also be crafted to feature both of these techniques in a single work

Illus. 5-1 and 5-2. Two relief-carved signs by Dick Malacek, Weathertop Woodcraft. Above left is a residential sign. Above right is a family crest.

(Illus. 5-3). Hand-carved signs can simply feature the message in carved lettering, or they can be expanded with auxiliary carved ornaments and decorations, transforming the signs into eloquent works of art (Illus. 5-3 and 5-4). There are only a few woodcarvers around the country involved in commercial wooden sign work. The demand for their skills is quite substantial, and in turn they can demand good fees. However, only those possessing great skill coupled with speed can make a livelihood.

This chapter will provide "how-to" instructions for the beginner. You will also see inspiring examples of beautiful sign work produced by highly skilled, professional woodcarvers. The techniques for the beginner are essentially the same as those used over and over again by the accomplished professional. The key point is to design and plan your first sign simply, that is, so its level of complexity does not exceed your skills or your patience.

Tools

Tools required for making hand-carved signs can involve many different shapes and styles of chisels and gouges (available to woodcarvers) or just a simple few. A small set of carving tools (Illus. 5-5) is more than adequate for beginners, as well as most professionals. It is strongly recommended that at the start you make do with tools you already have. Obtain additional tools one at a time as you determine whether or not you really need them. Many a good sign can be carved with just an ordinary carpenter's chisel, a jackknife, and perhaps a gouge. Having all of the various sizes and shapes of carving tools isn't really as important as you may think. What is of major importance is to be sure that the tools you do have are extremely sharp. This matter cannot be overly stressed. Trying to work with dull tools will discourage a novice faster than anything else. The tools must be "razor-sharp"!

Learning how to carve and properly use the tools can only be achieved by actually carving. So, start with the tool(s) you have. You will be able to determine if other special tools must be purchased to perfect your own style of sign carving. There are many excellent books that will instruct you about the general and technical aspects of woodcarving. Look at a few books for the additional information you may need, but, most of all, devote your greatest reading and study to the chapters about sharpening tools.

Illus. 5-3 and 5-4. Two signs by master carver Douglas Williams. The one at left features both incised and relief lettering, and the three-dimensional art was attached.

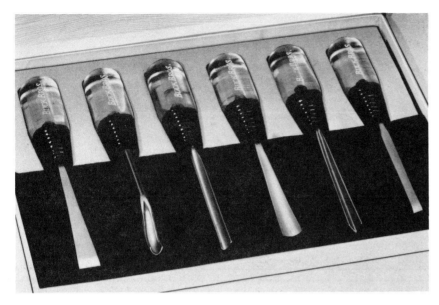

Illus. 5-5. A basic set of woodcarving tools.

You will find that to become a successful carver you must not only control the tool, but you must also control the response of the wood by anticipating how it will react to your cuts. You must know where and how much you want to cut away. Simply being able to accomplish this should be your first goal. Style, speed, and overall expertise will improve consistently with experience. Selecting good wood for carving is of major importance if you intend to control the wood's reaction to your efforts. At first it's assumed that all softwoods are the easiest to carve. This is by and large true, but softwoods require the sharpest edges—much sharper than for carving harder, denser woods. Dull tools will tear or crush the fibres of softwoods, and dull tools will require more force or energy when hardwoods are being carved. With properly sharpened tools, both softwoods and hardwoods alike will carve surprisingly easily.

In general, walnut, mahogany, basswood, redwood, and pine are good carving woods. For signs, particularly exterior signs, use redwood, mahogany, cedar, sugar pine, or basswood. Always purchase a select or high grade of wood. Be sure that it is free of knots, swirls, or cross grain. Your wood should have straight, uniform grain—especially for your first effort.

Carving

Carving will initially require continuous concentration with regard to grain direction. Later, this will become instinctive and you will be cutting automatically with the grain—simultaneously controlling the wood's reaction and your cutting tool. Cutting deeper than intended, or having chips come off where you do not want them to, can usually be traced to working against the grain or using dull tools.

Carving Incised Letters

The easiest kind of incised (carved-in) letters to make are those that are V-cut, so the deepest point is at the center of the letter. Attempting to carve out the total profile of the letter to a uniform depth is a very difficult task. To begin with, select a basic typeface, such as a simple block letter without fancy serifs (decorative tails). Plan the sign layout so that the letters run the length of the board, that is, so the majority of your cuts will be across the grain. You will find this easier than carving letters in which the grain runs vertically with the height of the letters. Use carbon paper and transfer your layout to the wood. Then draw a centerline on each letter to indicate where the deepest cut of the letter will be. End these centerlines with uniform triangles drawn at the end of the leg or the stroke of each character—connecting the centerlines to the outside lines. Study the layout in Illus. 5-6 and 5-7.

All woodcarving revolves around only a few basic techniques and kinds of cuts. The basic cuts are: (1) stop cuts (Illus. 5-6), which involve severing the fibres (usually across the grain), and (2) slicing cuts, which usually involve making cuts at an angle with the grain—moving the tool towards the

Illus. 5-6. *The centerline depth-cut is made first. Here, the gouge used to sever the grain fibres matches the curve of the letter.*

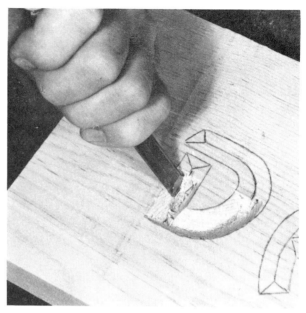

Illus. 5-8. *The straight "legs" of the letters can be made entirely with a carpenter's wood chisel. Note that the bevel is up for this sloping cut.*

Illus. 5-7. *The first slant cut begins to make one of the sloping sides of the letter.*

Illus. 5-9. *Nearing the final depth.*

stop cuts to remove chips (Illus. 5-7 and 5-8). Make the centerline depth-cuts first. Use a regular flat chisel for straight-line work. Hold it vertically with the cutting edge on the centerline and give it a firm blow with a mallet or hammer. The purpose of this cut is to sever the grain fibre. Then, subsequent slicing cuts can be made from each side toward the stop cut. If the stroke of the letter is curved rather than straight, you will need a gouge that matches the curve of the centerline, as in Illus. 5-6.

After the initial stop cuts have been made, make the slanted slicing cuts carefully, lifting out the chips (Illus. 5-7). Continue the vertical stop cuts, followed by the slicing cuts (Illus. 5-9) from each side until the desired depth is achieved. End the stroke (or leg) of the letters with triangular incisions. Use a sharp knife or chisel, and slice-cut these carefully (Illus. 5-10 and 5-11). Taper the cut from the centerline towards the outer end points.

Use a sharp knife to clean up the sides of the letters. Make certain that the deepest point is in the center of the letter and that all letters are cut close to a uniform depth. Do not sand the surfaces of the sloping sides. This will round off the sharp edge between the sign surface and the cut surfaces of the letter. Edges should be well defined— sharp and crisp.

Some chisel or gouge marks can be left intentionally to give the authenticity of hand-carved work (Illus. 5-12). However, if your objective is smooth-surfaced letters (as shown in Illus. 5-13), then remove all tool marks with light finishing cuts, using very sharp tools and taking the necessary time.

Illus. 5-10 (above left). A utility knife completes the sloping, tapered cut from the centerline to the outside corners. Illus. 5-11 (above right). An ordinary wood chisel can be used to clean up the sloping triangular end-cuts. Note that the bevel is up.

Illus. 5-12. The tool marks left by the carver, Pudge DeGraff, lend an authentic look and add character to this sign.

Illus. 5-13. An expertly crafted sign, carved about 30 years ago by an old German woodcarver, now deceased. Note the smooth surfaces of the letters.

Carving Raised Letters

Raised letters (relief work), as shown in Illus. 5-3, 5-4 and 5-14, are carved with essentially the same basic cuts used to carve incised letters. In relief work, the object is to remove, to a reasonably uniform depth, the wood surrounding the letters. If you want to produce a perfectly smooth, flat, and true background, you will become involved in a tedious and time-consuming job. Leaving tool marks on the background is acceptable as long as the overall appearance suggests uniformity over the entire background. This leaves a textured surface that serves as an interesting contrast to the smooth, undisturbed surface of the letter face (Illus. 5-14). Perhaps most important, textured backgrounds are faster and easier to carve.

Begin the carving by outlining the letter with vertical chisel or gouge cuts to sever the grain fibres. These cuts can be made more cleanly and easily (especially in softwoods) if they are not cut exactly vertically, but are made at a consistent, slight angle of about 5 to 10 degrees (Illus. 5-15). Outside curves can be cut with close, successive passes of a straight-edged chisel. Inside curves can be made with a curved gouge—preferably one with an edge that curves less than the curve of the letter. After the letter has been outlined completely, lift out the background with a chisel (Illus. 5-16) or gouge (Illus. 5-17), as appropriate. Always do this with slicing cuts, working with the grain. A bent gouge is helpful in cleaning up the background as shown in Illus. 5-18, but not absolutely necessary. Study Illus. 5-19—5-22.

Illus. 5-14. Relief lettering and art carved in redwood. This sign measures three feet by four feet. (Designed and carved by Bill Schnute.)

B

D

Illus. 5-15. Begin relief work by outlining the letters with slightly off-vertical cuts. Note that the bevel of the chisel faces away from the letter.

Illus. 5-16. Lifting out a chip with a regular carpenter's chisel—the bevel is down.

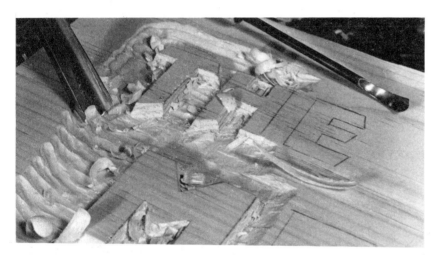

Illus. 5-17. Using a gouge to work away the background.

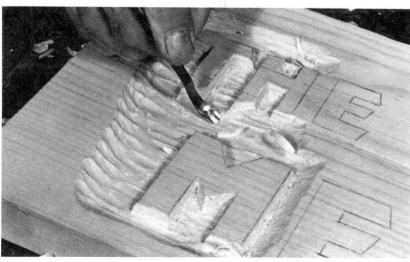

Illus. 5-18. A bent gouge (or bent chisel) is handy for levelling "tight" background spaces (between letters and so on). Here it is used to texture the background, emphasizing the tool marks.

Illus. 5-19—5-22. Carved redwood signs by Bill Schnute. Note his heavily textured backgrounds and delightful design ideas.

Carving Round Forms in Relief

Carving round forms in relief can add considerably to the uniqueness of wood signs—be they rounded letter faces, rounded borders, or special designs with rounded edges. A simple practice exercise is shown in Illus. 5-26. Here the lettering was outlined with a ³⁄₃₂-inch veining router bit, but it could be hand-cut. The convex face of the letter is being shaped entirely with an ordinary carpenter's wood chisel. However, other chisels, gouges, or knives could be used with the same results. Rounding over relief forms is a fairly easy job. With a little practice and some sanding you will be able to produce shapes similar to the details in

Illus. 5-25, 5-27, and 5-28. Once you round over simple designs, you are ready to include more details by making shallow incision cuts on these rounded surfaces to produce simple three-dimensional carvings. With practice, continual effort, and the desire to improve your carving skills, you will soon want to move on to the types of signs sculpted and embellished by professional carvers such as Bill Schnute, Dick Malacek, and Douglas Williams. Carefully study the hand-carved signs in Illus. 5-27 and 5-28. If you analyze these signs, reducing them to simple individual elements, you will note that they are actually not that complicated. With care, effort, and the basic techniques described above, you can carve them too.

Illus. 5-23—5-25. More of Douglas Williams' work for your inspiration.

Illus. 5-24.

Illus. 5-25.

Illus. 5-26. Using a chisel (bevel down, here) on a practice exercise for making convex-faced letters.

Illus. 5-27 (above left). An effectively designed carved wood sign. Illus. 5-28 (above right). This is a truly outstanding sign. At first glance it looks very difficult to execute, but study each character—are they as hard to carve as they seem?

Some Shortcuts

So far we have only explored the idea of producing authentic hand-carved signs, that is, those fashioned by physical labor with hand tools. Stock removal can be faster. Use a router or power rotary tools such as files and burrs driven in drill chucks, or flexible shafts. Not only can a lot of roughing-out time be saved, but not much thought needs to be given to grain direction. V router bits can be used to rough-in incised carved letters and knock off the outside corners of relief work to be rounded over. Finish all surface cuts with hand chisels and gouges to quickly create the hand-carved look. Similarly, letters can be outlined and

deep backgrounds removed with a router when doing relief work. Touch up the surfaces by hand, leaving the tool marks obvious. Carve by machine. Letters and other designs can be copied easily with carving duplicators. (Refer to Chapter 7.) Don't pass up the idea of combining hand-carved work with routed or sandblasted work on the same sign. See Illus. 5-29 for one very elementary example. Use whatever means you have to get the effect you want without expending excessive time or labor—that is, unless your efforts are done strictly as a labor of love.

If after all this you still find yourself not wanting to expend any efforts at all to make wood-carved ornaments, buy them. Wood mouldings and deco-

Illus. 5-29 (left). The background was routed away and then the surface was textured with a gouge. Illus. 5-30 (above). Just two of the hundreds of designs in wood mouldings and ornaments that can be purchased to decorate signs.

rations in numerous sizes, shapes, and design motifs are available. Simply glue them on. Imagine what you could do with the pre-carved ornaments shown in Illus. 5-30. One word of caution: Be sure that embossed carvings which are made of veneers are adequately sealed when used on exterior signs. Otherwise, they may delaminate (separate) unless they were originally manufactured for exterior conditions.

Another idea in this same vein is to be alert for aluminum, brass, or plastic castings of three-dimensional objects. Exterior, serviceable plaques (with flat backs) of birds, eagles, fish, animals, and many other designs are available in most hardware stores. When attached to your wood sign, they might provide just the ornamental touch you are looking for.

6

Routed Signs

The portable electric router, featuring great versatility coupled with a high cutting speed, lends itself perfectly to wood sign work of all kinds and sizes. It takes just a touch of know-how, a little imagination, and a bit of practice. You will quickly have the necessary skills, so there is no limit to what you can do. Very beautiful signs can be cut freehand and/or with the aid of various simple homemade (or inexpensive) guides that direct the router along its intended path.

Small name signs and very large commercial signs are routed in basically the same way (Illus. 6-1–6-4). Routed signs can be made with the letters either cut into the surface or raised above. Letters carved into the surface are called *engraved*. Engraved letters can be of uniform or various widths (Illus. 6-1 and 6-2). In the latter case, letters are cut by making multiple router passes with narrower bits. A form of engraved lettering is

"single stroke" work. In this class of work the width of the letter face is equal to the cutting diameter of the bit. The letter strokes are made in just one cutting pass or single carving "stroke" with the router (Illus. 6-2–6-4).

Raised or Relief Signs

Raised or relief signs have their background cut away. See Illus. 6-5 and 6-6. With a little practice, you can produce relief work with textured backgrounds that look as if they were carved by hand. You can also create other unusual effects of your own—simply by accident, or by plan. Look for other ideas to copy in addition to those shown here.

A specific kind or size of router cannot be recommended because personal needs, preferences, and budgets vary. We all know cheap electric tools

Illus. 6-1. An engraved, routed sign. Note how the letter strokes, or "legs," vary in width.

Illus. 6-2. A sign that combines engraved letters (with legs of various widths) and freehand single-stroke routing.

Illus. 6-3. A name sign in single-stroke routing cut with a round-bottom bit.

ıllus. 6-4. A big sign executed with a 1-inch-diameter round-bottom bit.

Illus. 6-6 (right). Raised (relief) work, cut entirely with the router using a round-bottom bit, simulates a hand-carved look.

Illus. 6-5. This routed sign, at a Florida development, makes excellent use of engraved and relief letters with a decorative design. (Designer and fabricator unknown.)

will neither last as long nor take the abuse that more expensive ones will. Tools with higher horsepower are heavier than those with less power. If you put your mind to it, you can learn to rout signs with any router. Investing in quality router bits is perhaps more important than buying a top-line router. After all, the bits do the cutting.

One thing I like about my router is its weight. It is big and heavy. Secondly, it has both a pistol-type handle and a knob located low on the base. Thus, I can press my hands and forearms down against the work to maintain good control of the router (Illus. 6-7). I also like the trigger switch. It's on the handle, so I can use it without moving my grip. My router will also carry two different sizes of collet chucks—¼ inch and ½ inch. The latter, along with the high-horsepower motor, allows me to use heavier, industrial-quality bits that cut deeper without vibration or chatter.

Illus. 6-8. A view of my homemade base. Note the rounded edges.

Illus. 6-7. The large hole of this router provides easy viewing of the cutting area.

My router lacked two features that I found a definite need for, and so I added them myself. The first feature is a transparent plastic base (with rounded lower edges) with a large center hole (Illus. 6-8). I used the factory-made base as a pattern and cut new ones of lexon and polycarbonate plastic. Use tough, clear plastics if you elect to do this, too. Acrylic plastic is a poor choice because it scratches and does not stay clear. Rounding the edges of the base allows the router to glide over slight protrusions and fibres that may be sticking above the surface of a sign-in-progress. The rounded base edges are especially appreciated when I'm routing rough-sawn surfaces and the surfaces of edge-glued panels.

The second feature is a vacuum attachment—a powerful, effective one. It is unhealthful to continually breathe that fine dust. Moreover, chips, dust, and freed particles get in the way. I devised a crude but workable attachment, attached directly to my shop vacuum with a hose. (Illus. 6-9 shows a

Illus. 6-9. This Craftsman Router has a self-contained dust bag. It has plenty of power and features a work light.

router with dust bag designed as part of the router. This product is great for keeping the dust under control.) Connecting the hose to the base unit of the router took a little effort. I cut a sheet-metal pipe reducer somewhat obliquely to fit alongside the router base.

A router with a light that illuminates the work area is a plus. My shop is well lighted so it's not a serious problem for me. You must always be able to see your layout lines clearly to know where you are cutting. I know several professionals, and they all have different brands and sizes of routers. Each is pleased with his own and wouldn't change—but one thing they all have in common is that they produce great signs.

Router Bits

Router bits should be selected for the shape, size, and kind of cut you intend to make (Illus. 6-10). If you can afford carbide bits, use them. You may at some time want a bit specially ground with which to make certain unusual cuts.

Freehand-routing Engraved Signs

Freehand-routing engraved signs does take some practice, but you will soon be able to expertly do it. At the end of this chapter you will find ideas for some guides that help the router in its work, but sooner or later you will have to try freehand routing.

Safety first! Use goggles, ear plugs, respirators, or whatever else is necessary to protect your own well-being. Be sure to clamp your work to the bench. Routing is best done as a "sit-down" job. This will save your back. Have an appropriate seat or stool at a height that allows you to have a good, almost level, "inside" view without straining your back.

Install your bit. Set the depth (Illus. 6-11). To start your first try, use a shallow depth (about ¼ inch or less) and a narrow straight-bottom bit (¼ inch or less is recommended). Greater depths can be cut with second passes. A shallow start makes router control easier. Stay with shallow depths until you get the feel for various stroke directions and different grain resistances.

Tilt the router, resting it on the base, with the bit clear. Turn on the power and pivot the router downwards, dropping the bit into the wood near the layout line. Outline the insides of the letter first, staying well enough away from the layout line in case you are a little "shaky" at the start. You can trim-cut up to the line later, after the "meat" of the letter has been removed. Analyze which direction the router tends to go when cuts are directed across, parallel with, and obliquely to, the grain. Study Illus. 6-12. This drawing indicates the recommended feed directions for making vertical and oblique trimming cuts close to the line. Cutting in directions opposite to those shown may cause the bit to grab and suddenly dig in, forcing you to go beyond the intended line of cut.

VEE-GROOVING BIT
For making Vee shaped grooves and beveling edges. Available in ½" diameter to cut ⅜" bevel and in 1¼" diameter to cut ⅞" bevel.

CORE BOX BITS
For cutting half circles and concave quarter circles. Available in ½" diameter.

VEINING BITS
For cutting round bottomed grooves and small concave corner edges. Radii on the end of the bits are ½ the bit diameter. Available up to ¼" diameter.

Illus. 6-10. Router bits and cuts.

STRAIGHT BITS
Plain bits with straight cutting edge for general routing—Straight square edges, dadoing, and small rabbets. Available up to ¾" diameter.

VEE CARVING BIT
Double end 45° Vee on one end, 60° Vee on other end.

STRAIGHT TYPE SINGLE FLUTE BITS FOR STRAIGHT ROUTING
Carbide cutting edges last 15 times longer than high speed steel on abrasive materials such as plywood, chipboard, and masonite®. Available up to ½" diameter.

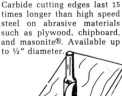

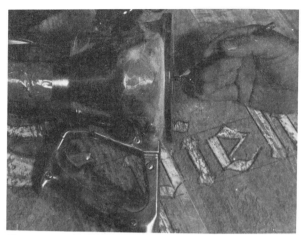

Illus. 6-11. A shallow depth and narrow bit are best for the first freehand-routing attempt. Note that the layout is chalked in to clearly indicate what needs to be cut away.

Illus. 6-12. The recommended feed directions for trimming (finish) cuts are shown by straight arrows. Bit rotation is indicated by curved arrows. Note that the grain is running horizontally.

The ideal rate or speed with which you move the router varies with bit sharpness, bit diameter, depth of cut, wood hardness, grain, and your eye—hand motor skills. Slowing to a near stop will cause the bit to burn and puff up some smoke. Don't fret! Take it easy and slow, carefully following the lines and gradually speeding up to a suitable feed-speed as you develop confidence and skill.

Be especially careful with small letters like o's, e's, and a's, so you don't "kick"-cut the center parts. It's for this very reason that small-sized letters are more difficult to rout than larger ones. Letters smaller than 1½ inches in height are likely to cause many more problems than 2- or 2½-inch

letters. Also, with small letters you will need to use narrower bits. When possible, rout from a previously cut area towards new wood. Routing towards and into an already cutout area is likely to cause the router to surge, and chipping or breaking off at "short grain" areas will result. See Illus. 6-13. For letters such as T's, L's, and E's, do the vertical strokes of the letters first, moving the router perpendicular to the grain direction. Finish the horizontal "bars" of the letters, going with the

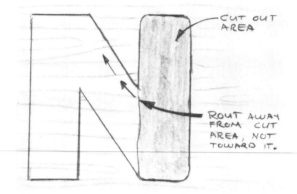

Illus. 6-13. When possible, feed away from previously cut areas, not towards them.

Illus. 6-14. An engraved initial plaque with routed edge.

Illus. 6-15. Engraved directional sign. Notice the dovetailed arm post.

grain. This procedure will minimize chipping at intersections. More examples of engraved letter work are shown in Illus. 6-14 and 6-15.

Sign Backings

With a Template

The projects shown in Illus. 6-16 can be made with either a fixed-base or plunge router. It is an ideal way for you to gain experience with template-routing. To make the sign plaque, cut the profile for the outside shapes with a template pattern and pierce through or just recess the heart designs, as you prefer, with the same template (Illus. 6-18–6-23).

Freehand-routing a Sign

Freehand routing is any cut made without the guidance of a device or some mechanical means to control the direction of the router. Accessories such as edge guides, straightedges, fences, tem-

plates or template guides, or special jigs and piloted bits *are not used* in freehand routing. It's just you and the router!

On some jobs it is impractical to use jigs. These jobs can only be accomplished freehand. Some types of freehand work are easier to do than other types. For example, it is difficult to completely cut a line that's part of a design in just one single pass of the router. It is not so difficult to engrave the letters in a signboard project. (See Illus. 6-24.)

There are many factors involved in successfully freehand-routing work. They include the following: (1) the size, style, and sharpness of the bit; (2) the type of router and its horsepower; (3) the characteristics of the wood itself; (4) the depth of cut; (5) the simplicity or complexity of the design; (6) the visibility of the bit; and (7) the physical strength of the operator.

Freehand routing can be fun if you approach it realizing that it takes some practice to gain the necessary skills. Expect to make some misdirected cuts.

Generally, you'll have more freehand-routing control if you use small-diameter bits with a heavy router that has more horsepower. Use carbide-tipped or solid carbide bits, especially when you have to feed the router slowly. In fact, sometimes it's almost easier to control slow, deep cuts than fast, shallow ones. If you feed slowly, as all beginners need to do, you'll overheat high-speed-steel bits and dull them quickly—much more so than carbide bits. Experienced freehand router craftsmen, however, will use high-speed-steel bits because they can be made very sharp. Experienced craftsmen also feed the router very quickly into the workpiece, and prefer to work with materials such as redwood, which machines easily.

Most router sub-bases are not ideally suited for freehand work. Use a sub-base with a large central hole so that you can see what is going on all around the bit. You may elect to remove the fac-

Illus. 6-16. This sign was template-routed.

FULL-SIZE LETTER PATTERNS

1" GRID SQUARES

FORM EDGES AS DESIRED

PEG LOCATIONS

2"

4¼" APART

Illus. 6-17. The plan for the signboard, in half scale. ("Half-scale" means that what is shown is half the size of the actual project.) The "welcome" letters are full-size patterns that can be cut out with a scroll saw and applied to the signboard.

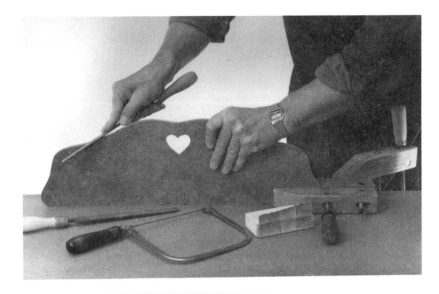

Illus. 6-18. Make the template with a scroll saw. Then smooth away any dips or irregularities on the contoured edges. This template, used for making the signboard, is being touched up with a file.

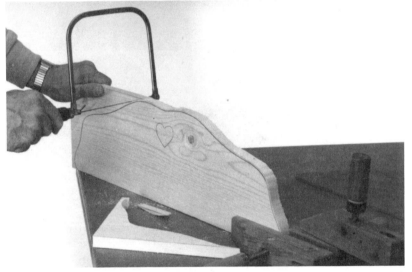

Illus. 6-19. Saw the project to its rough size, about ⅛ to ³⁄₁₆ inch from the layout lines. The very rough cut left by this crude coping saw is of no consequence as long as the project is cut oversize.

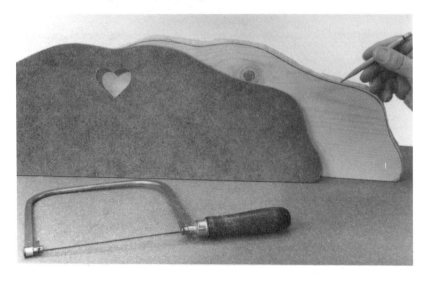

Illus. 6-20. A look at the signboard template and the rough-sawn blank.

Illus. 6-21. Secure the template to the rough-sawn blank with double-sided tape or strategically placed spots of hot melt. Then prepare the template and workpiece to be trimmed with a hand-held router. Nails tend to get in the way of the router base, even if they have been driven into the back of the workpiece, so use a couple of pieces of double-faced tape to hold the template against the workpiece for routing.

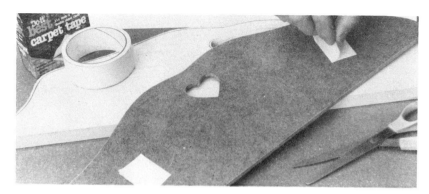

Illus. 6-22. Before trimming the template, clamp the work so that the cut is made over the edge of the workbench. Then make the trimming cuts. Note that the template pattern is under the project blank, and that the rough cut is being trimmed down to the template's exact size with a ball-bearing trimming bit.

Illus. 6-23. Trimming the workpiece. A close-up look at the cutting action. Apply pressure to the workpiece side of the router so that it doesn't tip. A base with a smaller opening would be better. This one does give us an unobstructed view, however.

Illus. 6-24. These engraved letters were routed in multiple passes. The design of the letters made the job easy. The lines of the letters did not have to be perfectly straight, uniform in width, or exactly identical to each other, yet the overall appearance and effect of the sign is good. (Refer to Illus. 6-39. for the letter patterns necessary to make this project.)

tory sub-base and replace it with a self-made version that provides maximum visibility. This is a situation in which it is nice to have a transparent plastic base.

Make some practice cuts in scrap before undertaking an important project. It's important that you know how the router feels and moves when it starts up, and when the bit passes through the wood in different directions to the grain.

Make sure you are set up comfortably. Generally, it's best to be sitting, but this actually depends upon the size of the job and the height at which you must work the wood. Illus. 6-25 shows how and where to clamp the workpiece on the workbench so that it is in the best location for routing.

Make practice cuts on the face of a piece of inexpensive softwood, such as pine (Illus. 6-26).

These cuts should run in different directions. You will quickly learn, as mentioned, that there are many factors that influence how successfully you make the cut. Two of these factors—the speed and rotation direction of the router bit—remain constant. Factors that constantly change, however, are the feed speed, the direction the router is moved, and the way the bit cuts in relation to the grain direction.

By looking at Illus. 6-26, you'll note that the router will stray away from its intended course and go in another direction when fed in different angles to the grain of the wood. Study this illustration so that you can anticipate what the router will do when you freehand-rout.

It's usually best to move the router in a direction that will tend to pull the router away from rather

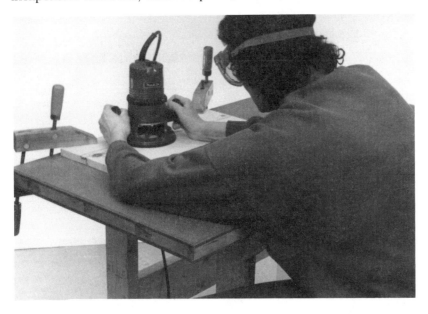

Illus. 6-25. Here is the proper way to freehand-rout. The workpiece is securely clamped and well back on the workbench, so that the operator's arms rest on the bench and are fairly outstretched. The operator is seated so that he has a good view of the cutting bit. Note the goggles. Always use goggles for any job.

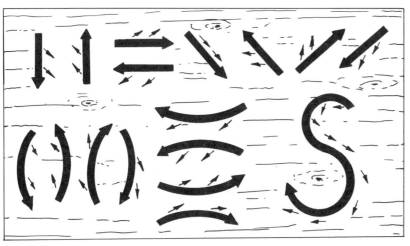

Illus. 6-26. Shown here are strokes you should practice, and the wandering tendencies of the router when it is fed in various directions in wood with horizontal grain. The large arrows are the intended feed directions. The small arrows indicate the direction the router tends to go if it is not physically restrained.

Illus. 6-27. This workpiece is ready for freehand routing. It is laid out with sharp, but dark, pencil lines and clamped tightly to the workbench. The factory sub-base is not being used. Instead, a special self-made sub-base designed to give maximum visibility around the bit has been substituted.

than towards or into a straight line. (See Illus. 6-27.) Also, try to make cuts from a top-to-bottom feed direction, that is, make a cut across a board by starting at the farthest point and pulling the router towards you. This is called a "downstroke."

It is easier to control a router by making a downstroke than trying to make the same cut by pushing the router away from yourself—called an "upstroke." You'll find that it is easiest to feed the router on a downstroke at approximately a 45-degree slant to the right. The router almost follows a straight line by itself in this direction. The most difficult feed is directly the opposite—an upstroke, 45 degrees to the left. Try to avoid this stroke whenever possible.

Although it's more time-consuming and slows the job, you can make better cuts by unclamping the board and reorientating it on the bench so that you can make most of the cuts with a pulling downstroke, rather than with a pushing upstroke.

Illus. 6-28–6-38 show and describe a technique for routing a typical sign with engraved-style letters. Essentially, the process involves making an initial narrow pass through the middle of the letter and then widening it with successive passes until you have routed to the layout line(s). The same process can be applied to rout out various other designs, such as hearts, animal profiles, etc. In all cases, first rough out the central area and then gradually increase the cuts, cutting little by little outward towards the layout line. You may need to make several slow final passes, all from the same direction, until all the waste is cut away.

You'll no doubt find occasion to repair a mis-cut, as shown in Illus. 6-35. You can often correct such mis-cuts simply by "fairing out" the line, that is, reworking and smoothing out the cut line so that it flows gradually back into the course of the original. (See Illus. 6-35–6-37.)

As you gain experience, you'll begin to move the router faster, with more confidence and skill. At this time, try some single-stroke work, such as outlining various designs in one continuous pass with the router, or routing letters in a single stroke.

Single-Stroke Freehand Work

In this class of work, letters are made quickly with one straight-line or smooth-flowing, curved stroke. Each stroke component (leg or curve of the letter) is completed with just one pass of the router. For example, the vertical of the letter *D* is made with one straight vertical stroke (top to bottom). The router is lifted and moved to the top and the curve of the letter is completed with a second

Illus. 6-28. Routing a sign with engraved letters. Set a ¼-inch straight-cutting bit at a cutting depth of ³⁄₁₆ inch. Make one pass down the approximate middle of the letter. Try not to touch the layout line.

Illus. 6-29. Slowly widen the cut by working on the left side of the previous pass with a down-stroke (that is, pulling the router towards you).

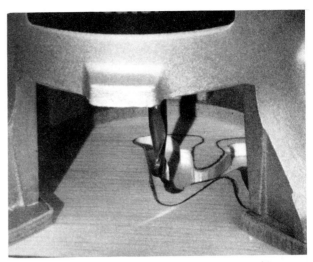

Illus. 6-30. Remember the following rule until you develop a "feel" for the cut: The maximum width of each successive stroke (pass) should not be greater than half the diameter of the bit.

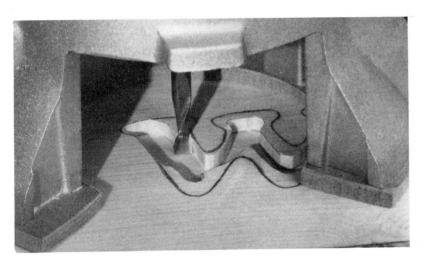

Illus. 6-31. To widen the cut, use as many strokes or passes as necessary until you meet the layout line.

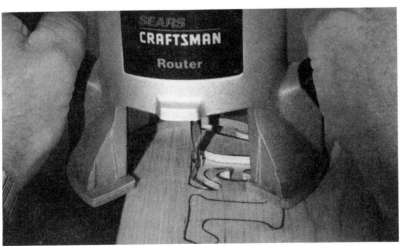

Illus. 6-32. Making a horizontal cut with the grain, on the bottom of the letter E. It's best to reposition the workpiece under the clamp so that you can use a pull stroke. Again, work on the left side of the previous cut, progressively working towards the left until you meet the line.

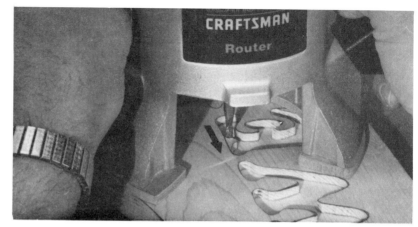

Illus. 6-33. Reclamp the workpiece or position yourself so that you can make horizontal cuts with a pull stroke, such as on the top of the letter E, as shown here.

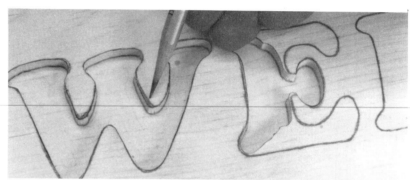

Illus. 6-34. Look at your work. If the cut is not widened all the way to the line but the overall shape of the letter looks good, then leave it as it is. Removing this slight uncut amount isn't worth the risk of cutting away more than intended.

Illus. 6-35. If you accidentally cut beyond the line, as shown here, you can rework the shape of the letter by "fairing it out." (See Illus. 6-36.)

Illus. 6-36. If you fair out the line with a new trimming cut, as indicated by the arrow, the outline of the letter will appear smooth and flowing again.

Illus. 6-37. The touched-up letter may not be perfect, but it is definitely improved visually and will not stand out. You can fair out almost all lines, whether they are curved or straight.

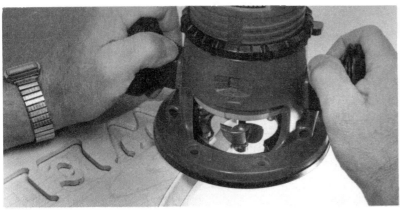

Illus. 6-38. Complete the sign routing by forming a decorative edge all around the outside with a piloted bit. This class of routing is far more foolproof than freehand work.

single pass. Some examples of single-stroke routed signs are shown in Illus. 6-40–6-43. Once skilled at this, you can rout a small sign in 3 to 5 minutes. This skill will come with practice.

A less rigid style of lettering is the best to start with. See Illus. 6-44 for a suggested style. Note that all of the straight cuts are not perfectly straight and the curves are not uniform compass-type curves. A good layout, however, is still essential—especially for the beginner. With some effort you can learn to lay out this style of lettering without any problems. Simply use chalk and the "trial and error" method. Lightly chalk it on, and if it does not look right or is not centered, wipe it off with a dry rag and do it again, making the necessary adjustments. Once you get it spaced out to a good-looking layout, darken and widen the chalk letters to a suitable width. Then outline the chalk lines freehand with pencil. See Illus. 6-45. Select a

router bit of the approximate corresponding diameter.

The round bottom or cove bits are effective for freehand single-stroke work. With this type of bit, a bumpy or irregular curve and straight lines can be smoothed or "faired" out. Of course, this requires making another pass over the same part of the letter, but this is preferable to letting a sloppy job go by. This slightly increases the width of the letter face at the corrected area. Unless it's extremely bad in the first place, the corrected letter is usually indistinguishable from the others. With more experience and practice, you will have less correcting to do.

You will find it best to press down on the router handles and reduce the speed of feed when you anticipate that the router might be pulled from your intended direction. This is likely to occur around or when going through knots, from heart-

Illus. 6-39. You can enlarge these letters and numbers on a copy machine to make any size sign desired.

Illus. 6-40. A freehand, single-stroke routed sign. Lettering was cut with a round-bottom bit, and the art was cut with a V-bit.

Illus. 6-41. This small business sign was routed freehand.

Illus. 6-42 and 6-43. House number and name signs made by single-stroke, freehand routing.

Illus. 6-43.

AABCDEEFG
HIJKLLMMN
OPQRRSSTUV
WWXYZ
1234567890

ABCDEFGH
IJKLMNOPQ
RSTUVWX
YZ&
1234567890

Illus. 6-44. Alphabets for single-stroke routing. The single-line, freestyle letters are easy to lay out and rout freehand. The double-line letters require more skill.

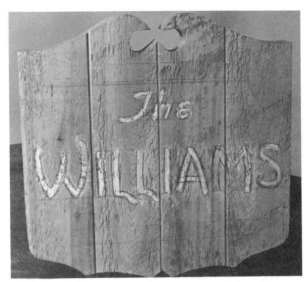

Illus. 6-45. A chalked layout has been outlined in pencil for freehand, single-stroke routing.

Illus. 6-47. V-bits with different angles and diameters.

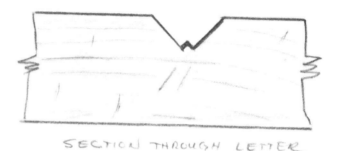

SECTION THROUGH LETTER

Illus. 6-48. This inverted V will result if correction-cuts are made with a V-bit.

wood to sapwood, with other changes of grain direction, and just before coming into another cut. See Illus. 6-46. You will learn to use your wrists as "compass arms." You will soon be able to let the router basically glide itself "downhill" *with* the grain, and restrain it with just the right pressure as you move it "uphill" *against* the grain. The same old principles are involved in almost all forms of routed sign work—practice and more practice!

Freehand single-stroke routing with V-groove bits (Illus. 6-47) requires greater skill because cor-rections, if necessary, are more noticeable. Unless you increase the depth of cut, a "telltale" inverted V (as drawn in Illus. 6-48) will appear at the center of the letter. Consequently you cannot widen the edges of the letter stroke one at a time. Both must be done with one new stroke and the bit set deeper. Remember, the deeper the cut, the more difficult it is to maintain control. Most sign-carvers use redwood when using V-bits. Its easy-cutting and very uniform grain are more consis-tent from piece to piece than any other wood. An advantage of a V-bit is that the cutting width can be changed quickly by raising or lowering the depth of cut. Hence, a different bit need not be installed with every change. Very professional effects with serifs and decorative swirls (swashes) on the ends of letters can be produced (Illus. 6-49—6-51). These are made by lifting the router as you complete the stroke. To accomplish this requires not only router practice, but also a knowledge of type styles to which this effect is suitable.

Routing Aids

If you have come this far without mastering the

Illus. 6-46. Freehand, single-stroke routing. Note that the work is firmly clamped down and is completely on the bench to allow the forearm and wrist to control the router.

Illus. 6-49. A truly professional job of single-stroke freehand routing in redwood. (Crafted by the Old Oak Shop.)

Illus. 6-50 (above left). A close-up look at the "tail" shows that the cut gradually becomes shallower at the end of the stroke. Illus. 6-51 (above right). Another sign by the Old Oak Shop. Note the simulated checks and end-splits cut with a V-bit. The art was outlined with shallow cuts, and then artistically hand-painted.

ups and downs of freehand work, do not despair. There are some homemade and inexpensive devices that can be used to help you make beautiful engraved and raised letters.

Straightedge

A **straightedge** is the simplest of all guides. Although a true straight line is perhaps the most difficult to cut freehand, it's very easy when the router is pushed along a straightedge. The straightedge must be clamped or nailed parallel to the line of cut. Locate the straightedge a distance from the line of cut that equals the distance from the router bit's cutting edge to the edge of the router base (Illus. 6-52 and 6-53). So you don't have to always measure this distance, rip a "spacer stick" from ¼- or ⅛-inch hardboard or plywood (Illus. 6-52). Use the spacer stick to line up the straightedge the appropriate distance from the

line of cut as shown in Illus. 6-54. The proper feed direction of the router is important. Feed the router from the direction that tends to pull the router towards the straightedge. This is shown in

Illus. 6-52. A "spacer stick" is ripped to a width equaling the distance between the bit's cutting edge and the edge of the router base.

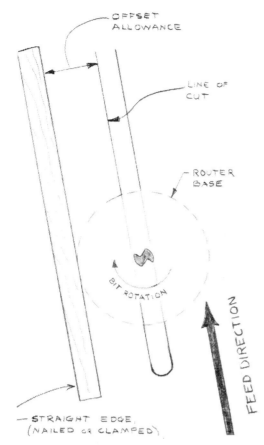

Illus. 6-53. The location of the straightedge as it is positioned along the line of cut. Note the recommended direction of feed.

Illus. 6-54. Positioning the straightedge with the help of the spacer stick.

Illus. 6-53. When feeding in the direction opposite to that shown, the rotation direction of the router bit tends to force the router away from the straightedge. This tendency, of course, can be overcome with physical pressure, but you must apply pressure continuously throughout the entire cut.

Use the straightedge for uniform alignment in cutting the tops and bottoms of all letters that have straight-line strokes (Illus. 6-55 and 6-56).

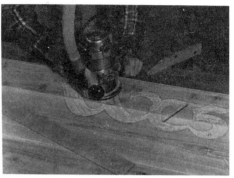

Illus. 6-55. Making a cut by following the straightedge ensures that the line of this letter will be perfectly straight.

Illus. 6-56. Here the straightedge, nailed to the sign, ensures that all letters will be cut to identical heights.

T-Square Guide

A **T-square guide** is another easily made fixture. It is used to make straight-line vertical cuts in letters that are perpendicular to the bottom or base line. The device simply consists of two parallel straightedges (¼ inch in the thickness) spaced equally apart at a distance that equals the diameter of the router base plus ¹⁄₆₄ inch for clearance. The "head" of the T-square is made of ¾-inch plywood so it can hook over the bottom edge of the sign (Illus. 6-57 and 6-58). This double straightedge T-square guide allows you to feed the router in either direction without fear of the router straying away from the line of cut. When clamped securely, the straight-line angle cuts of *N*'s, *A*'s, etc., can be made without problems (Illus. 6-65). The remaining curved strokes of the letters must be completed freehand (Illus. 6-60 and 6-61).

Illus. 6-57 (above left). A T-square designed for guiding the router. Here a spacer stick is used to position the T-square properly along the line of cut. Illus. 6-58 (above right). The T-square is used here to make true vertical cuts for the outline of a large letter.

Illus. 6-59 (above left). The straight-line slanted legs of letters can be cut in the same manner with the T-square guide firmly clamped. Illus. 6-60 (above right). Once all of the straight-line horizontal and vertical cuts have been made with the straightedge and T-square, the curved cuts must be completed freehand.

Illus. 6-61. A completed sign in which all straight lines were cut with the aid of a straightedge and T-square. Other cuts were made strictly freehand.

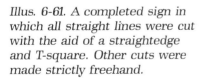

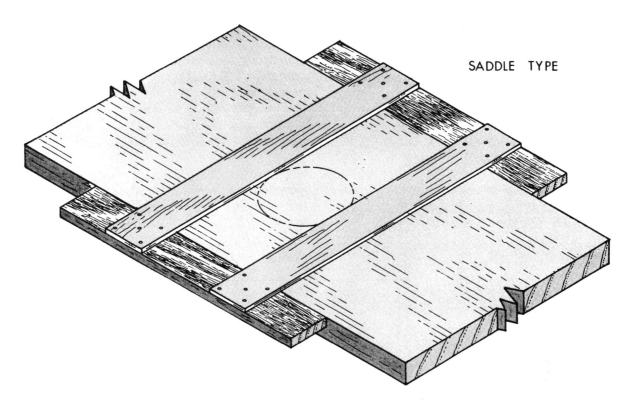

SADDLE TYPE

Illus. 6-62. A saddle-type straightedge is made to fit a specific board or panel width, as shown here.

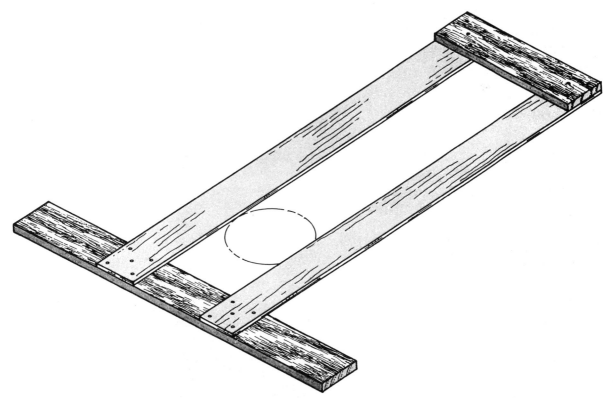

Illus. 6-63. Here is another double straightedge that can be used on stock of any width, narrow or wide.

Routing Perfect Circles

Routing perfect circles is especially difficult to do freehand. Often large signs require true circular cuts with a uniform radius, such as those shown in Illus. 6-64 and 6-65. This kind of work can be done easily if you use a compass routing device with your router. The device consists only of one piece of ¼-inch hardboard (or plywood) made to fit onto the base of the router as shown in Illus. 6-66. Use a nail for the compass pivot point (Illus. 6-67). Set the nail at the center of the circle, tap it in, and make the cut feeding from either direction (Illus. 6-68 and 6-69).

Illus. 6-64. The perfect circular design on this sign was cut with the aid of a compass routing device.

Illus. 6-65. All of the curved cuts of this logo are perfectly circular and were made with the simple device shown in Illus. 6-66—6-69.

Illus. 6-66. The compass cutting device is made to be mounted to the base of the router.

Illus. 6-67. A nail makes the pivot point for the center of the circle. Position the nail so the radius of the cut is from the outside of the bit's cutting edge.

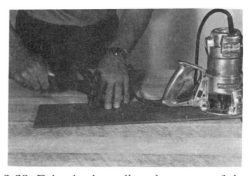

Illus. 6-68. Drive in the nail at the center of the circle.

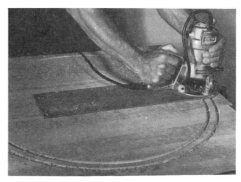

Illus. 6-69. Making perfect circular cuts. Note that parallel circular cuts can be made easily.

Letter Routing with Templates

Engraved and raised letters or other characters (including perfect small and large circles) can be made simply by tracing templates with the router. The templates can either be purchased or made yourself from ¼-inch plywood or hardboard. One item you need is a template routing guide (hollow bushing) that fits into the center hole of your standard router base (Illus. 6-70). Most router manufacturers provide these in sets with various size openings so that you can use bits with various cutting diameters. The template guide bushing protrudes through the bottom of the plastic router base and bears against the letter template during the routing operation.

Illus. 6-70. A close-up view of a homemade letter template and the relationship of the template guide and the router bit.

To make raised letters, nail the template directly to the sign (Illus. 6-71). Once you have installed the proper combination of router bit and template guide bushing, set the bit to the desired

Illus. 6-71. Templates nailed in place for making raised letters.

depth. *Caution:* Be careful when lowering the rotating bit into the work. Be sure you do not accidentally cut the template with the bit. Follow along with slight horizontal pressure so that the template guide always rides against the template during the outlining operation. Turn off the router and wait for the bit to coast to a complete stop before lifting the router.

The same general idea can be employed to make engraved letters. Or, you can purchase a template set made especially for this type of work, as shown in Illus. 6-72.

Illus. 6-72. A template-holding device for routing engraved letters. Sold by Sears (model 2573), this setup has 58 plastic templates with heights of 2¾ inches and 1¾ inches, and it comes with a clamping system. It is low-cost and easy to use.

Making a Square Base

Make your square base from hardboard, plywood, or plastic that is about ¼ inch thick. Use the sub-base that has come with your router as a pattern for the hole-mounting locations in the sub-base you are making. Make your base the size you want, so that it will provide four different distances from each edge to the bit (Illus. 6-73).

If, for example, you are using a ¼-inch-diameter bit, make the distance from one edge to the bit one that's easy to remember, such as exactly 3 inches. Make one of the two adjoining edges ³⁄₁₆ inches from the bit, and the remaining two edges 3⅛ and 3¼ inches from the bit. Mount the base to the router, and check its four cutting distances on scrap wood.

Your router now has the capability of making four different cuts at four different distances off-set from a guiding straightedge. The line of cut will depend upon which edge of the base is selected to guide the router.

Using the T-Square Guide

Illus. 6-74 shows how an engraved cut can be quickly widened, using the same bit, a T-square guide, and a router with a square base. A different edge of the base is used with each successive pass of the router.

If you prefer to cut more or less material per pass, you'll have to plan and make your base accordingly. You may decide, for example, to make a very fine second trimming cut, one that's a mere ¹⁄₃₂ inch, or even ¹⁄₆₄ inch. To do this, you only have to orientate the router position and make the trimming pass rather than reset or move the straightedge or guide over this small distance.

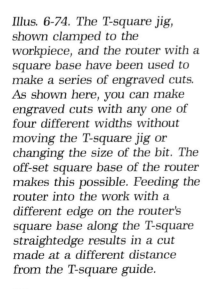

Illus. 6-73. The existing sub-base shown on the left provides the mounting-screw-hole pattern for the square base. Note that the center hole (and the bit) will, by design, be off-set different distances from each of the four edges.

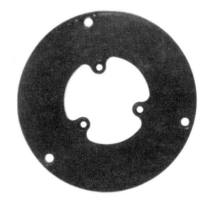

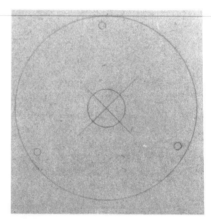

Illus. 6-74. The T-square jig, shown clamped to the workpiece, and the router with a square base have been used to make a series of engraved cuts. As shown here, you can make engraved cuts with any one of four different widths without moving the T-square jig or changing the size of the bit. The off-set square base of the router makes this possible. Feeding the router into the work with a different edge on the router's square base along the T-square straightedge results in a cut made at a different distance from the T-square guide.

Illus. 6-75. The off-set distance is the distance from the cutting edge of the bit to one of the selected edges of the base.

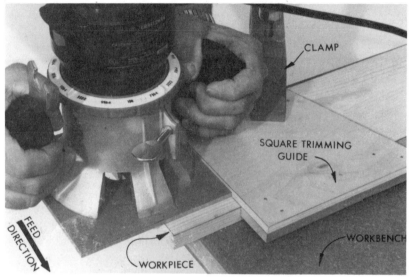

CLAMP

SQUARE TRIMMING GUIDE

FEED DIRECTION

WORKPIECE

WORKBENCH

Illus. 6-76. Using a router with a square base and a square-trimming guide. Clamp the guide the distance it should be off-set from the end of the board so that you can make the light trimming-cut exactly where desired.

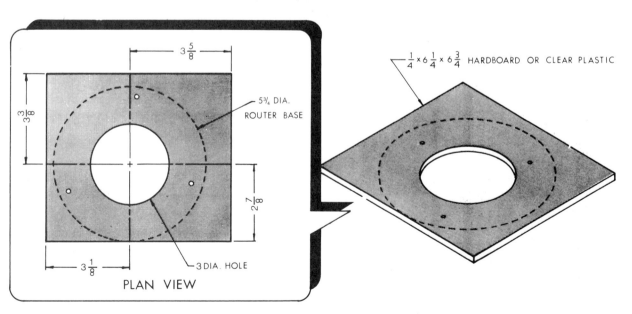

$3\frac{5}{8}$

$3\frac{3}{8}$

$5\frac{3}{4}$ DIA. ROUTER BASE

$2\frac{7}{8}$

$3\frac{1}{8}$

3 DIA. HOLE

PLAN VIEW

$\frac{1}{4} \times 6\frac{1}{4} \times 6\frac{3}{4}$ HARDBOARD OR CLEAR PLASTIC

Illus. 6-77. Suggested details for making an off-set router base. This idea can be applied to widening engraved letters.

7

Sign Routing and Carving Machines

This chapter briefly describes some of the sign-making machines currently available on the market. Most equipment of this type is based upon a template-guided router that reproduces the exact letter shapes of the master patterns. They are, in fact, copying machines. They can be operated without any previous woodworking experience and do not require any special artistic skills. The machines vary in price, from fifteen dollars up to over one hundred. In most cases, the templates, guides, bits, and other accessories are extra, and with some machines the buyer must also provide or purchase the router power unit separately.

Any bit carried by a conventional portable router can be used with this type of equipment. Round, square-bottom, or V-bits are used to produce various signs. Letters and/or decorations are either carved into the surface (engraved) or raised by cutting away all of the background. Some manufacturers offer very complete sets of templates in a variety of type styles with upper- and lowercase letters, spacers, numerals, special characters, and even three-dimensional design motifs.

A cutout letter can be made using a sabre saw, band saw, or router. The problem is where to get the patterns. Sears has two sets of patterns that are the right size for most applications. They are ideal for signs requiring 6- to 10-inch-high letters.

Illus. 7-2. These five signs contain the type of letters provided in the Sears model 2518 Stencil Set. Styles are: Modern Writing, Far East, Script, Computer, and Old English.

Illus. 7-1. The Sears Wood Sign Kit has Old English and block style stencils.

96

Another set of letters that can be used for cutout letters is in the Sears model 2518 Stencil Set. This product was designed for use with a router pantograph shown in Illus. 7-4. Five styles are included with upper- and lowercase letters and numbers. These letters are done with a nice touch for cutout or engraved letters. Carbon paper is not included, but you can transfer these letters as you did those in the Sears model 25176 Wood Sign Kit.

Modern Writing letters look best routed with a V-groove bit. The deeper you set the router bit in the wood, the wider the groove. For the other four styles of letters use a ⅛-inch-diameter straight-face bit. Cutout letters can be made in Old English, Script, Computer, and Far East. Simply transfer the letter to the wood with carbon paper and saw it out with a sabre or band saw. Rotary Pantograph model 26003 is available through the Sears *Power and Hand Tool Catalog* (Illus. 7-3). Sears rotary tools can be used to engrave small signs and plaques in wood. Bushings are included to adapt other models.

The engravings are always reduced in size from the patterns at a percentage of 40, 50, or 60 percent. Using a 3-inch letter stencil, engraved signs can be made 1¼, 1½, or 2¾ inches high because of this reducing ratio. Almost perfect results can be achieved on the first try.

To use the pantograph, guide the stylus on the line of the stencil and engrave the image at a reduced size with the rotary bit. When you lift the stylus, the cutting bit is raised out of the wood; this is necessary to move to inside lines. Lower the stylus on the inside line and proceed.

It is recommended that V-groove bits and pointed cutters be used with the pantograph. These bits will give maximum detail for line art when cutting shallow, or a wider line when set deeper. If a flat-bottom letter such as Old English is desired, use a small, straight flat-bottom bit.

Deluxe Router Pantograph

The Deluxe (3-D) Router Pantograph (Illus. 7-4) is also available for sign-making and three dimensional carving. This pantograph is constructed of heavy steel tubing and a foam-moulded adapter plate needed to perform the 3-D functions. Standard equipment includes five sets of letter and number stencils and a pair of wedges to hold the workboard. An easily made fixture will help greatly in making signs. Dimensions for making this fixture are in the pantograph's instruction sheet (Illus. 7-5).

Signs of any length can be made using a panto-

Illus. 7-3. This pantograph is used with Sears rotary tools. It is available in the Power and Hand Tool Catalog *as model 26003. Signs or line-art drawings can be reproduced on wood quickly and easily.*

97

Illus. 7-4. A partially completed sign in Old English using the Sears model 25187 Router Pantograph.

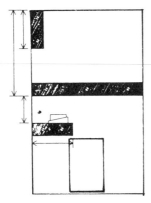

Illus. 7-5. This is a fixture you can create to aid you when making signs using the Router Pantograph.

Illus. 7-6. A variety of sign designs and artwork similar to that which can be made using the Router Pantograph. (Photo courtesy of Kimball Carving Machine Co.)

graph. The board is simply moved along under the router as you continue to develop the sign one letter at a time. For special effects and beauty, line drawings can be engraved later on the ends.

Three-dimensional work requires a pattern to follow. Plaster castings and plastic plaques are inexpensive patterns that can be used for 3-D engraving. These are usually available at most crafts, hardware, and department stores. With the Sears Pantograph, patterns up to 12 × 24 inches and 1¼ inches thick can be reproduced. When glued on, they add decorative embellishments to routed wood signs.

Use a small round-nosed cutter for fine detail work. Sears has ⅛- and ³⁄₁₆-inch veining bits which are ideal for this type of intricate carving. The eagle in Illus. 7-7 was engraved in eight hours.

Rout-A-Signer

The Rout-A-Signer (Illus. 7-9) produces engraved, slanted (about 28 degrees) block letters. This sign-making machine (available at Sears outlets) is adjustable, producing letters from ¾ inch to 4½ inches in height. It must be combined with your own router. Signs of any length can be made, but stock is limited to 10 inches in width and boards ½ to 2 inches thick. In operation, plastic templates are traced with a stylus which, by means of a steel bar linkage, moves the router.

It comes partially assembled, with operating instructions and 58 templates of 1½- and 2½-inch numerals and uppercase block letters in a plastic

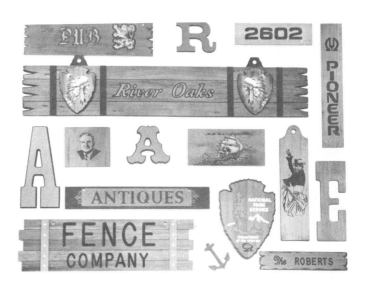

Illus. 7-7 (far left). Here, the Sears 25187 Router Pantograph proportionally reduces a plaster pattern for a three-dimensional wood sign decoration. Illus. 7-8 (left). The wedges are shown holding the workpiece using the fixture in Illus. 7-6.

Illus. 7-9. The Sears model 2572 Rout-A-Signer.

storage carousel. No template guide (bushing) is required for the router base. The router adapter (to which your router is attached) is made of polystyrene plastic. Other parts are steel. The total weight is approximately 10 pounds. The overall size, assembled, is 30 × 22 inches, and 2½ inches high.

Miniature Sign Layout Kit

The Miniature Sign Layout Kit has over 100 stencils in three letter styles. Cutout letters such as those shown in Illus. 7-10 and 7-11 can easily be carved out, using a scroll saw and this kit. Spacing and location of letter centerlines are part of each

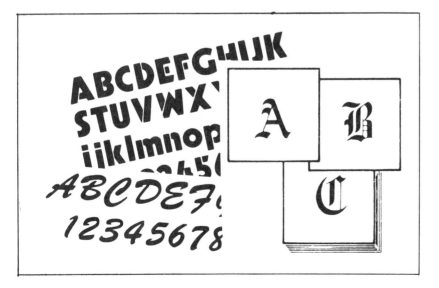

Illus. 7-10. The Sears model 25196 Miniature Sign Layout Kit has three styles of letters and numbers: Script, Old English, and block styles 2, 3, and 4 inches high.

stencil to help you do good work. For a desk sign such as "Bonnie" in Illus. 7-11, you can leave each letter attached at the bottom. By cutting the bottom at an angle, the letters will be slanted back for a nice effect. Sizes of letters are 2, 3, and 4 inches.

Rout-A-Copier

Often we have patterns of a letter and number style and want a full-size reproduction. There is a product at Sears that can be used with a router to do just that, make full-size reproductions (Illus. 7-12). Using the **Rout-A-Copier**, you can produce a full-size engraving using patterns of letters, numbers, line drawings, and even a finished sign as a master. Plunge routers are easier to use with this machine. A three-step process is used. In the first step, you trace the desired image on the upper

Illus. 7-11. Beautiful hand-carved signs can be made using the Miniature Sign Layout Kit. Shown here is one sign in each of the three styles. The "Bonnie" sign is in Script letters 3 inches high. It is cut in mahogany for use as a desk sign. The "Sign Kit" sign is cut all the way through, and was laid out in Old English. The "Sears Craftsman" sign is in block letters. The "Sears" is engraved in, and the "Craftsman" is left standing by engraving around each letter using a router.

Illus. 7-12. The Rout-A-Copier, model 25126. This is a router accessory for reproducing wood engravings from the pattern on a one-to-one scale.

lens. In step two, you follow the traced image by locating the router between the lens and the workpiece, and then rout the engraving. In step three, you finish the sign as desired. The router bits recommended for use with the Rout-A-Copier are V-bits and small straight face bits. These types of bits will give maximum detail to the finished product.

All routers with a flat top can be used with the Rout-A-Copier. There are a few routers that have a cord that comes out of the top center. These routers cannot be used with the Rout-A-Copier.

When making wood signs using the router or scroll saw, it is helpful to keep your hands on the tool or workpiece. A foot pedal such as the one shown in Illus. 7-13 is an aid for the signmaker. Being able to control the on-off switch with your foot is especially desirable when you are using the pantographs and Rout-A-Copiers. Using the foot pedal with the scroll saw to cut out letters and numbers is also convenient.

Illus. 7-13. Foot pedal, model 25172. The on-off foot switch is used on tools that draw up to 15 amps on 115 V.

8

Making Large Signs

Larger signs are laid out, routed, hand-carved, or sandblasted the same way as smaller signs. The problems associated with making larger signs include: (1) making or preparing large panels, which requires some equipment, (2) making joints, and (3) using fasteners that are required to assemble signs and hang them on buildings or from posts.

As mentioned in an earlier chapter, plywood can often be used for the background panels of large signs. Plywood does not lend itself to hand-carving or sandblast carving. Sometimes, however, plywood can be used for signs that are to be engraved with the router, providing you use carbide bits. Large sheets of plywood framed with solid wood borders add to the depth and overall rigidity of the sign. Some ways of making borders for plywood panels are shown in Illus. 8-1.

When solid lumber is glued together to make large sign panels, it is seldom framed unless the

framing members are part of the sign-post assembly (Illus. 8-2.) If edge-to-edge glued sign panels of solid wood are to be framed, be sure to

Illus. 8-2. This large sign (6-foot-square face) is made of edge-glued 2-inch-thick planks, set and glued into grooves cut into 6-inch-by-6-inch timbers.

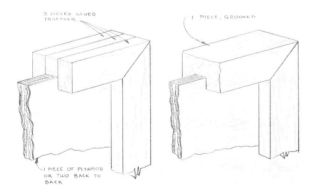

Illus. 8-1. Making borders for plywood signs.

allow space for expansion. Otherwise, the corner joints of your frame may separate. See Illus. 8-3. As a general rule, avoid framing large edge-glued solid panels because of wood's tendency to expand and contract with changes in environmental humidity. See Illus. 8-4.

Preparing and Gluing Panels

Preparing and gluing panels for larger signs involves some generally common woodworking practices. Begin by selecting your lumber for boards of uniform thickness. Incidentally, 2-inch thickness is best for large signs. If the sign is to have a smooth surface, you will get the best results if the boards are all run through a thickness planer. If only one face of the sign needs to be left with a rough-sawn surface, then these boards also can be run through the thickness planer, removing stock from the least desirable face or side of each

board. Before surfacing rough-sawn wood, it is a good idea to touch-sand it (Illus. 8-5). Arrange the boards so that defects, such as knots, end up away from the lettering area. Once arranged, chalk a triangle onto the face sides (Illus. 8-6). This will enable you to get them back quickly into the predetermined sequence. Smooth and square the edges with a power jointer or carefully with a hand plane.

If the signboards are longer than 2 feet, they should be doweled in their joints. The purpose of doweling is more a matter of alignment than adding strength to the joint. Often, long boards will be bowed along their length. The dowels used in edge-to-edge gluing will bring each edge into alignment with the edge of the board next to it, and will also keep the edges in the proper positions until clamping pressure is applied. This will ensure a flat, uniform sign face. Doweling begins by drawing lines across the dowel locations (about

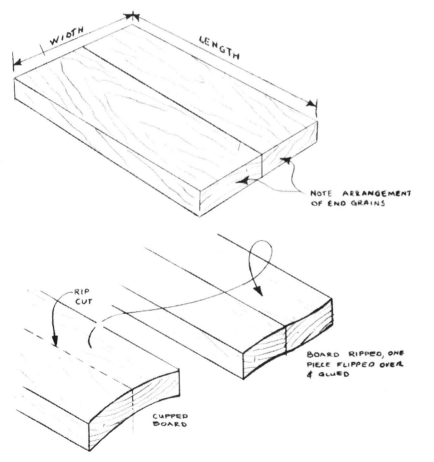

Illus. 8-3. Solid wood glued edge to edge to make large sign panels. Remember that wood swells (and shrinks) considerably in width and very little in length.

Illus. 8-4. Wide planks tend to warp or are warped at the start. Ripping and then gluing them back together makes them stay flatter.

Illus. 8-5. Touch-sanding rough-sawn surfaces improves the surfaces for planing, gluing, and subsequent routing. The sanding levels fibres and other irregularities, especially around knots.

Illus. 8-6. Gluing arrangement of the planks is marked with a triangle to identify the gluing order.

Illus. 8-7. Marking for dowels is best done by drawing the line on both edges of the joint at the same time.

Illus. 8-8. A self-centering dowel jig. A mark on the jig corresponds to the center of the dowel hole.

Illus. 8-9. A wooden block under the chuck ensures that all holes will be drilled to the proper depth.

6 to 12 inches apart) along the edges of the adjoining boards, as shown in Illus. 8-7. Use a dowel jig to ensure that the dowel holes are drilled vertically and are exactly centered across the edge (Illus. 8-8 and 8-9).

On signs that have rough-sawn surfaces, it may be desirable to emphasize the joint. This is accomplished by making a slight chamfer cut along each board edge on the face side. The result is a neat, inverted V when the joint is brought together, as shown in Illus. 8-10. The chamber cut also ensures that the router base will slide easily, without interference, over the joint. Often, the edge of a board is slightly higher (or lower) than the board next to

Illus. 8-10. A slight chamfer, cut at the edge and face-corners of each board, will emphasize the glue joint and make routing easier.

Illus. 8-12. The chamfering operation can be done with a piloted chamfering router bit (as shown) or with a hand plane.

it, as shown in Illus. 8-11. Problems can arise when you are routing sign faces that have these irregular surfaces. Usually the router base strikes a high edge and causes a frustrating miscue. Uneven surfaces, such as shown in Illus. 8-11, can be sanded down only if the sign is to have a completely smooth face. The chamfering operation is shown in Illus. 8-12.

Glues for exterior signs should be selected very carefully. Too much work goes into signs of this type to have them ruined just because the wrong glue was used. A resorcinol-resin glue is often recommended for completely waterproof glue joints. It comes as a liquid and a powder, and must be measured carefully and mixed together. It leaves a distastefully wide and reddish discoloring stain along the glue lines. It's also expensive. I don't like it and can't understand why it is always "the" recommended glue. I use a marine-grade, powdered, plastic resin glue formulated for boat builders. It leaves a glue line that is almost colorless and barely detectable. It is much less expensive than any resorcinol I have priced. It has a long shelf life (in a tightly closed container), sets in 4 hours,

cures overnight, and can be used at a lower temperature than resorcinol. This glue mixes with water and, before it sets, it can be cleaned up with water. Epoxy glue is very good. Though it's messy to work with and expensive, epoxy (and resorcinol) glue adheres even when wood is submerged at length in boiling water. A one-part, ready-to-use liquid glue under the "Tightbond Waterproof" label, manufactured by Franklin Adhesives, is now available. It is easy to use, clears up with water, and can be found in most hardware and woodworking supply catalogues.

Spread the glue (of your choice) to the edges (Illus. 8-13) and drive in the dowels (Illus. 8-14).

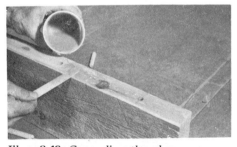

Illus. 8-13. Spreading the glue.

Illus. 8-11. If unchamfered edges stick up, routing is more difficult.

Illus. 8-14. After the glue has been spread, drive dowels into one board of the joint. No special effort need be made to get the glue on the dowels or into the holes.

Don't waste time trying to get glue on the dowels and into the dowel holes. Remember, the dowels are only used to assist the alignment in assembly. Dowels add little strength to the joint. Most woodworkers will tell you that the glue joint is stronger than the wood itself. Apply clamping pressure (Illus. 8-15). A good joint should have some glue squeeze-out. However, be careful when working with rough-sawn planks. Excessive glue will be difficult to get off. Use a putty knife (Illus. 8-16) to lift and clean the squeezed-out glue from the joint area. This is generally easy if you have the V-groove at the joint. See Illus. 8-17. A very light sanding, after the glue has cured, will make an excellent routing surface. Obviously, if you are using smoothly surfaced planks, most of the above procedures and precautions need not apply.

Sometimes you may elect to use steel rods (continuously threaded) running through the sign to pull the boards tightly together (edge to edge). These are available in all hardware stores. Use those that are zinc-plated, and also use zinc-plated washers and nuts. Reinforcing your sign

Illus. 8-17. Final cleanup is made with a damp rag.

with steel rods is a good idea, especially if the sign is to be a free-hanging type (Illus. 8-18 and 8-19). The steel rods will keep the pieces of wood together should one of the boards eventually split lengthwise. Running steel rods is more difficult than it first seems. The holes must be drilled exactly through the center. If a hole is slightly off, or if one of the boards is cupped, you may create a seriously distorted and bowed face when drawing the nuts up tight. A dowel drilling jig is often helpful for starting perfectly centered holes. Drill in from both edges of each board, going as deeply as you can with the dowel drilling jig. Usually it is a good idea to counterbore a large hole about 1½ inches deep at the outside edge. This will allow you to hide the washer and nut with a wood plug, dowel, or wood filler. See Illus. 8-20 and 8-21.

Illus. 8-15. A sign glued and clamped. Note the use of clamps both above and below the sign. The scrap blocks under the clamp jaws distribute pressure and prevent crushing at clamping points.

Illus. 8-16. Lifting the excess glue from the V-joint of a sign assembled from rough-sawn edge-glued planks.

Illus. 8-18. A free-hanging sign made of three pieces of rough-sawn wood, joined edge to edge.

Illus. 8-19. This double-faced sign measures about 3½ feet in diameter. It is made of smooth-faced wood with eyebolts coupled to steel rods that run vertically through the sign.

Illus. 8-22. This large sign fabricated by Spielman's Cedar Works consists of 2 × 8 planks glued edge to edge.

Illus. 8-20. This special tool is handy for counterboring operations.

Illus. 8-21. This plug cutter makes dowel pins from scrap. They can be made with grain running either way.

Screws eyes or lag hooks are used to hang small and medium-size signs. The bigger the sign, the bigger the fasteners you need. Remember, fasteners driven into the board's end grain do not hold very well. Consequently, signs to be hung, such as those shown in Illus. 8-23 and 8-24, should have a suitable anchor. Since screws hold better when inserted across the grain rather than with the grain, use a large dowel anchor as shown in Illus. 8-25.

Often the sign's boards and blanks need to be fastened directly to posts, as shown in Illus. 8-26 and 8-27. They can be fastened directly from the face side. The fasteners can be concealed with plugs to give a pegged effect (Illus. 8-26 and 8-27) or concealed with flush plugs (Illus. 8-28).

Posts for small name signs can be made in several ways. Three different ideas are shown in Illus. 8-29–8-31. These pictures are essentially self-explanatory as far as construction details are concerned. Posts for any kind of sign should be of a material that has a high resistance to decay, such

Illus. 8-23. Hanging this thick, heavy sign will require well-anchored hooks on the top.

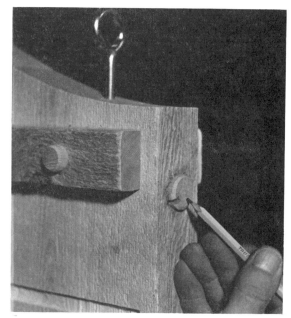

Illus. 8-25. This dowel (glued) makes a strong anchor for the screw eye above, which is driven into it.

Illus. 8-24. A sign to be hung. The screw eyes are driven into the end grain of the vertical planks.

Illus. 8-26. The sign planks are fastened from the face to the posts with hidden lag bolts. Dowel plugs conceal the bolts and add to the overall character of this rustic sign.

Illus. 8-27. This large single-faced sign is 4 inches thick, and measures about 36 inches by 72 inches. It is glued, lagged, and plugged to two 8-by-8 posts.

Illus. 8-29. A single-faced sign can be mounted directly to the post.

Illus. 8-28. These planks are attached to the posts with lag screws, which are concealed by plugs inserted flush to the surface.

Illus. 8-30. A post with a horizontal arm for hanging a sign must be strongly constructed so it does not sag.

Illus. 8-31. A round pole that has been flattened on two sides makes an interesting post for this double-faced sign.

as redwood, cedar, cypress, or pressure-treated timbers. In cold areas of the country where frost lift can be a problem, be sure that the post(s) is long enough, and the hole dug deep enough, to get below the frost line. If you plan to cement the post(s) in, make your hole with a larger diameter at the bottom of the hole than at the top. This dovetails the post and concrete into the ground. Consequently, it will be much more difficult for the frost to lift it out.

Posts for larger, commercial-type signs should be of a suitable proportional size so they are not overbearing, yet appear to be strong enough, and are strong enough. Some thought must be given to the best height for the sign. Consider ditches, future weeds, or brush growing up in front of the sign. In northern areas, deep snows and plowed banks could cover sign faces if the signs are installed too close to the ground. One of the easiest post systems to fabricate is shown in Illus. 8-32. Multiple posts can add greatly to the overall design effect. See Illus. 8-43—8-45 for some post designs and construction ideas for supporting large signs.

Illus. 8-32. A post structure for a large sign is made with simple lap joints, bolted together.

Illus. 8-33. Four-by-fours cut so the sign panel comes through to the outside make an easy-to-build but substantial-looking post system.

Illus. 8-34 and 8-35. Two views of an interesting sign in Florida. Note the low sign and the decorative use of round poles, which have been left at random heights, as posts. The close-up of the sign face shows the effectiveness of lettering routed to two different depths. (Designer and fabricator unknown.)

Illus. 8-36. The post structure not only supports the informative sign but also "frames" the entrance to this park.

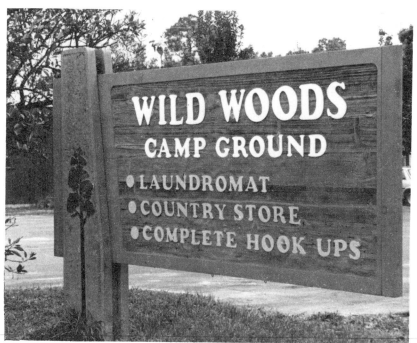

Illus. 8-37. This unusual sign features sandblasted designs on the posts, which are made of two large planks. (Designer and fabricator unknown.)

Illus. 8-38. A double-faced sign by Spielman's Cedar Works has identical panels face-mounted to two vertical posts.

Illus. 8-39. The extra posts give needed mass for the visual sense of support and strength.

Illus. 8-40. Smooth redwood sign and sculpture complemented with stone. Sign is 6 inches thick and measures 12 inches by 14 feet. The sculpted design is 12½ feet long and its thickest point is 2½ feet.

Illus. 8-41. A sign designed for portability. The customer wanted to be able to move the sign without leaving postholes in the blacktop parking lot.

Illus. 8-42. Large, heavy hanging signs must be anchored to prevent wind sway. Six-inch-square posts support this sign, which is securely chained at top and bottom.

Illus. 8-43. This massive sign was made by gluing 2 × 6's layer upon layer so that their edges become the face of the sign.

Illus. 8-44. Another massive sign made of horizontally layered 2 × 6's.

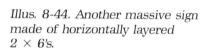

Illus. 8-45. This massive sign by Spielmans Wood Works features hand-carved letters and a boat in very high relief with carved rope border. The sign measures 5 × 11½ feet and is 5½ inches thick. It was made by glue-laminating 4 × 6 timbers together.

9

Making a Huge Sign

In this chapter the major steps involved in producing a huge sign are illustrated and described. This one example is included to offer proof that there is virtually no limit to wooden sign work. How big is big enough to be considered "huge" is perhaps a matter of opinion. However, the sign fabricated in this chapter has the following general specifications: The sign face is 7½ feet wide by 10½ feet high and it is 4½ inches thick (solid). It takes six men to lift the sign alone. The sign post structure consists of 2800 board feet of timbers. The timbers are set 4 feet below ground level and anchored with 11 cubic yards of concrete.

The size of this job and equipment involved appear at first more than you want to undertake. However, the extra tools (clamps, etc.) can often be borrowed or rented. You can also find someone to subcontract the work that you cannot handle yourself. Ask around for help before turning down the opportunity to do a challenging and satisfying job such as shown here. Remember, making a huge sign involves the same principles as a small sign—it just takes longer and everything is on a larger scale.

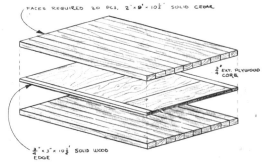

Illus. 9-1 (left). The sign just after it was hung. It measures 4½ inches thick, and is 7½ feet by 10½ feet. The sign is double-faced and is router-carved with raised lettering. Twenty-eight hundred board feet of hand-hewn posts (4 feet below ground) support the structure along with 11 cubic yards of concrete. Illus. 9-2 (above). The sign face is totally glue-laminated with edge-to-edge glued planks. The thickness is built up with an exterior-grade plywood core with solid wood for the core edges.

115

Illus. 9-3. The face panels. The first panel (standing) is already glued and cut, and the second panel (in long pipe-clamps) is being edge-to-edge-glued on the workbench.

Illus. 9-4. Levelling the gluing surfaces by cross-grain sanding.

Illus. 9-5. The profile shape cuts are made before glue-up. The one face is used as a pattern to cut the second face.

Illus. 9-6. The hanger eyes are imbedded and anchored to the interior of the sign during glue-up. This ¾-inch-diameter steel rod and eye is welded to a steel plate (⅜ inch thick, 3 inches by 16 inches), screwed and epoxy-paste-glued into the pocket cut into the ¾-inch plywood core.

Illus. 9-7. Preparing the glue on the last face. At this point the core has already been glued and nailed to one face. Note the solid wood at the edges of the core.

Illus. 9-8. Clamps are placed around the outside edges. The total thickness was completed in a single glue-up.

Illus. 9-9. A total view of the thickness glue-up. Timbers are wedged against the ceiling to apply pressure to the center of the sign—pressing it to the workbench.

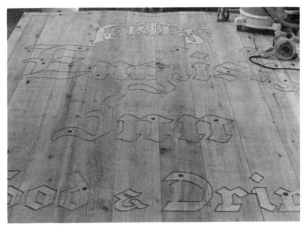

Illus. 9-10. The sign laid out, ready for routing—note the router and vacuum in the corner. The dark circles on the letter faces are holes where lag bolts were driven in during the gluing operation. The holes are later filled with plugs, set flush to the letter-face surfaces.

Illus. 9-11. The author about to begin routing. A ¼-inch round-bottom bit will be used to outline all letters, cutting only to a shallow depth.

Illus. 9-12. A close look at the router-carved raised lettering. A 1-inch-diameter carbide round-nose bit was used to remove all of the background, cutting ⅞ inch deep. Routing was done with the grain, stopping the strokes right at the shallow-cut, outlined letters. Routing away the background consumed 72 hours alone.

Illus. 9-13. A model (scaled at 1 inch to the foot) was made to check the right visual look for the post structure.

Illus. 9-14. The posts (made of 12-inch-square timbers) were cut, fitted, and hand-hewn, and brought to the construction site for final assembly.

Illus. 9-15. The post assembly is braced, lifted, and set into the holes with a forklift.

Illus. 9-16 (above left). The structure is levelled vertically and horizontally. The heavy equipment holds it plumb as the concrete sets in the holes. Illus. 9-17 (above right). The forklift hauled the sign from the shop to the site and made easy work of hanging it on the post structure.

Sandblasting Signs

The cutting or etching of wood signs by sandblasting is not a new technique. *Signs of the Times* magazine ran articles introducing some basic techniques in the 1930s. The process of impelling abrasive particles with a high-pressure air system actually originated in Great Britain in 1870. Today, because people are tiring of metal, plastic, and neon, sandblasted signs are in vogue. Modern equipment, easy-to-cut stencils, and the growing demand for unusual wood signs (large and small) provide the sandblasting sign-maker a new, easy, and growing medium in the field of wood signs. Sandblasted signs are beautiful, distinctive, and unique.

Essentially, this abrasive etching technique is the same process used to engrave names, art, and dates in granite and marble monuments— particularly tombstones. Engraving in wood is obviously easier and faster than sandblasting in stone, and the wood craftsman has much more latitude for creative expression. The process is relatively easy to learn. In fact, it requires much less skill and practice to blast a professional-looking sign than it does to carve one by hand or to use a router freehand. Its ease was proven by our 17-year-old exchange student. She produced the name sign shown in Illus. 10-1 in her very first attempt. The process is basically this: (1) adhere the stencil, (2) transfer the design, (3) cut the stencil, and (4) blast.

The sandblast process can be used to make raised letters (Illus. 10-1 and 10-2), engraved work, or a combination of both (Illus. 10-3). Further dimensional effects can be achieved by combining hand-carved or router-shaped designs and borders with your sandblasted creations. Built-up borders, attached carvings, or ready-made ornaments can be fastened to the sign to produce dramatic,

Illus. 10-1. Sandblasting signs is easy, as exemplified by this one in flat-sawn redwood. It was made by 17-year-old Lis Kukla without any previous experience.

Illus. 10-2. A small sign in vertical-grained redwood.

Illus. 10-3. This sign in rough-sawn cedar features engraved and raised sandblasted lettering and freehand router work.

Illus. 10-4. A house number in flat-grained western red cedar.

Illus. 10-5. Three boards of knotty flat-sawn cedar were glued edge to edge to make the width of this sign.

deep-dimensional signs of unparalleled appeal and individuality.

Woods for Sandblasting

A wide variety of different species can be used, but redwood is far superior to any other kind of wood in its desirable response to blasting. Cedar (the western red species) also responds well to blasting. White cedar is considerably tougher than red, but it can be blasted well with heavy equipment and additional time (Illus. 10-3 and 10-5). Mahogany, walnut, spruce, and pine also respond well to blasting. Some woods, although apparently soft, do not blast easily. They seem to be too "spongy." Willow and butternut are good examples. Although I have blasted these, they take three or four times longer than cedar or redwood and consume a proportionate quantity of additional sand to get the job done.

Woods can be glued together, edge to edge, to make large panels. See Illus. 10-5. There may be some irregularity in depth along the glue lines due to varying hardness or grain patterns at the joint. If you select stock by carefully matching the kinds of wood and the face-grain patterns, you should achieve a uniformly blasted surface regardless of the glue line.

Vertical Grain versus Flat Grain

Whether the wood has vertical or flat grain plays no part in the wood's response to sandblasting (Illus. 10-6). However, each results in its own unique blast-textured surface qualities. Vertical-grain boards will have very pronounced, thin, straight lines as typified by the sign shown in Illus. 10-2. This effect is the result of the softer, less dense part of the tree's growth ring being blasted away faster than the harder areas. See Illus. 10-1, 10-3, and 10-4, which show the texture of blasted surfaces resulting from boards having flat-grain faces. Remember that vertical-grain boards shrink and swell less than flat-sawn wood. They also do not warp as easily. On single-faced signs made from flat-grain boards, use the bark side of the board for the front as it will weather better than the pith side.

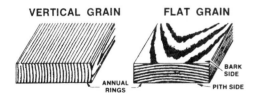

Illus. 10-6. The type of grain pattern on the sign face is directly related to the kind of textured surface obtained from sandblasting.

Knots

Knots in all species of wood do not blast away

easily, and remain higher than the surrounding area. This may or may not be desirable, depending upon your personal preference. To some of us, knots are as much a natural part of wood as the sun is a part of daylight, and they should be a part of the overall plan. However, large knots overlapping the edges of letters will diminish the clarity and crispness of execution. Consequently, knots, if allowed, are best planned to end up in the background areas. If high knots are objectionable after initial blasting, cut them down with chisel or router, and then blast the area again. Study Illus. 10-5.

Equipment

Your ability to blast various materials is related to the air delivery of your air compressor and the matching suitability of your sandblaster unit. Test various materials for yourself to see which one gives you the depth you want in the shortest time. We've experimented with and tested many kinds of materials. Our unusual experiment in particle board, shown in 10-7, proved to us that the potential for the sandblasting process has yet to be fully challenged.

Illus. 10-7. An experiment with sandblasted particle board.

The first step is to obtain the necessary equipment, or at least the use of it. It's very expensive, and it would be foolish for the amateur to buy the equipment without first gaining some experience and intelligent technical assistance. The essentials are: (1) an appropriate air compressor, (2) a sandblaster (also called a sandblast generator or

121

"pot"), and (3) the masking material commonly referred to as sandblast stencil or tape.

If you know someone in the tombstone and monument business you will get a lot of help and information. Also check the Yellow Pages for sandblasting services, and talk to people in auto body repair and finishing shops where they use sandblasting to remove rust and old finishes. In fact, it would be a good idea to engage one of these services to blast your first sign—that is, assuming you are not already equipped with some sort of compressor and sandblaster. If you look around hard enough and are somewhat lucky, you may be able to purchase small quantities of the necessary supplies from one of the above businesses. Try your best to buy some stencil and adhesive from a monument carver. If all your contacts fail, check out the equipment rental agencies in your city—many do rent portable compressors and sandblasters. With the appropriate equipment a small sign (10 by 24 inches) in redwood can be blasted in 15 to 20 minutes maximum. Consequently, it would be much more practical to take your first signs to someone with the equipment, rather than moving the equipment to your shop for only several minutes' work.

The equipment available for sandblasting today includes a wide range of sizes and optional features—all at various prices to satisfy your exact requirements and budget.

Air Compressors

Air compressors of the smaller sizes and capacities (often found in home workshops for occasional utility work) will not, as a rule, be satisfactory for you in the long run. If you have a compressor of the 1- to 1½-horsepower size, try it, but don't expect too much. Compressors of this size do not produce the quantity of continuous air delivery necessary for pleasurable blasting. As the horsepower on compressors increases, so does the amount of continuous air supply, and so does your delight in blasting. Compressors of 1½-hp will work, but you will soon be discouraged. Basically, compressor capacities are designated by horsepower (hp) and cfm (cubic feet per minute). Do not be misled by a compressor ad specifying a high psi (pounds per square inch). When you set the compressor to increase the psi, the cfm capacity becomes less. For example, a typical 3-hp compressor has a 6.9 cfm rating at 40 psi but drops to a 5.8 cfm when the pressure is increased to 90 psi.

You will find that most businesses using air to either lift a garage hoist, sandblast car bodies, or operate air tools will have at least a 5-hp compressor. Wood signs can be sandblasted (with redwood as the standard) satisfactorily with a 3-hp unit, easily with a 5-hp unit, and very quickly with the 7½- to 10-hp units that the professionals insist upon. Thus, the rate or speed at which you can blast or etch away wood varies directly with the species of wood and amount of air supply—but most directly with the latter. Our compressor is a 7½-hp unit with a 24.6 cfm rating at 175 psi. This is more than adequate. A 5-hp unit with an air delivery of 15 to 18 cfm at 175 psi would be ideal for most serious wood-blasting craftsmen. Remember, high psi is not a major factor in sandblasting—you will get good results with 35 to 80 psi as greater pressures are seldom required. Continuous air supply is most important. The air requirements are also dictated by the kind of sandblasting unit and the size of the nozzle opening.

Sandblasters

Sandblasters (Illus. 10-8–10-10) range from economy models to high-production machines. As a rule, sandblasters are designated by required cfm of air in accordance with recommended hose sizes and nozzle diameters. Many optional fea-

Illus. 10-8. An economy sandblaster with 60-pound sand capacity.

Illus. 10-9. A larger unit with 120-pound capacity and wheels for portability. Both units have 3/32-inch air jets and 3/16-inch ceramic nozzles (both available at Sears).

Illus. 10-10. A pressure-type sandblaster features a water extractor and sand-control lever.

tures are available; some are used only occasionally, while others are almost a necessity for full-time operation. Professionals like larger sand-holding capacities so they do not have to shut down to load sand. However, this is not usually a major inconvenience with an average-size 150-pound pot. Sandblasters function in several basic ways. They all have a pot that holds the sand and various levers and valves to control the mixture of sand and air. Sandblasters can be categorized as either suction-feed or pressure-feed units. Suction- (or siphon-) feed units can operate on as little as 4 to 7 cfm of air.

The better blasters are the pressurized type, and they usually require at least a 5-hp compressor around the 25-cfm range. This kind of unit allows the use of a 1/8-inch-diameter nozzle opening and will consume approximately 100 pounds of sand per hour. Changing the nozzle size changes the cfm requirement. A smaller nozzle, such as 3/32 inch, requires about 11 cfm at 70 psi or 12 cfm at 80 psi. Unless you have ample space, or can afford a special indoor room or booth, you will likely be forced to do your blasting outside. It is imperative that your compressor be located (piped) a safe distance away from the blasting area so that the compressor's intake air is not contaminated with sand or dust particles. One desirable, highly recommended feature is a water extractor, which will eliminate many problems related to clogged valves, nozzles, and sand passages. There is always moisture in compressed air.

Nozzles for the sandblaster are made of materials that resist the abrasive nature of the moving sand. Tungsten carbide, boron carbide, and ceramic are good nozzle materials, with ceramic the most economical. Ceramic outwears cheaper cast-iron and steel nozzles.

Only your own experience, coupled with sound technical advice for your specific needs, will determine the best equipment for you.

Abrasives and Blasting Media

Abrasives and blasting media can include any granular material that will go through the filling screen of the blaster. Some cut faster, others have polishing effects, Dry beach sand, silica sand, glass beads, metal shot, garnet, silicon carbide, and aluminum oxide are typically used. They are the hardest and fastest-cutting abrasives, but they also accelerate wear to nozzles and other parts of the blaster. Silica sand is available at most building centers. Blasting abrasives are classified by a nominal mesh size (U.S. Sieve). Generally, the coarser the grit, the faster the cutting action. For most sign work, 40 to 80 grit is suitable. One hundred grit and finer is not recommended. Use the 40 grit for fast cutting on large signs where delicate detail is not so essential. Use 60 grit for the majority of your work on small signs.

Caution: Be sure to use suitable operator safety and protective accessories. Always wear a dust filter (respirator) that covers your mouth and nose. Prolonged breathing of dust may cause delayed lung injury (silicosis). A blasting hood (helmet) is also a must item for protection against rebounding abrasives. An inexpensive canvas hood with a viewing window and ventilation screens can be used for outdoor work. Outdoor blasting in large opened cardboard shipping boxes, plastic-covered crates, or similar improvised booths will allow you to reclaim some of the sand for reuse.

Stencil Materials

Stencil materials for sandblasting wood signs (Illus. 10-11) have in the past been essentially a soft rubber sheet material approximately $3/32$ to $1/8$ inch thick with a rubber-based adhesive backing designed especially for the marble and granite monument industry.

The major problem with these materials is that they are designed especially for the monument carver, not for wood sign sandblasting. They can be made to work, but their adhesives are formulated to adhere to the smoothly polished surfaces of marble and granite. Blasting in stone obviously requires a heavier-gauge stencil material than is needed for redwood.

Illus. 10-11. A roll of sandblast stencil. All have an easy-to-remove liner that exposes the adhesive-coated backing.

The most popular stencils used by wood sign blasters are 3-M 508 Gen. Purpose. Most come in rolls of 10-yard lengths with a width of 30 inches or more, but narrower sizes as small as $10\frac{1}{2}$ inches are available from at least one company. Small pieces can be butted tightly together to make full use of your scrap materials.

One company has made available a new rubber stencil material developed especially for blasting wood signs. This new product is called Signblast Tape, and it is manufactured by Anchor Continental, Inc., 2000 S. Beltline Blvd., P.O. Drawer G, Columbia, South Carolina 29250. Unlike the other stencils or masks previously used, this new material has a very aggressive adhesive tack. This feature makes it possible to use this tape on raw, unfinished wood without any auxiliary application of the contact cements (or fillers) that were previously necessary to assure good adhesion. These supplemental adhesives often left a sticky residue that was extremely difficult to remove from the raw wood.

One word of caution: The adhesive formula on the new stencil material may in fact be too aggressive for some soft woods and especially some prefinished panels. We have ruined several signs simply because we did not test first. For example, we were making some interior signs and had lacquered the surfaces before applying this new stencil material. After blasting we removed the stencil, removing not only some of the lacquer finish, but also chips and slivers. The finish that did stay on the panels pulled the adhesive away from the back of the stencil, leaving us with a combination of problems and a real sticky mess.

On the other hand, we have had simply excellent results when applying this new stencil to raw redwood, cedar, and pine. We have been somewhat successful using the new stencil on rough-sawn boards, too, but they must be touch-sanded first. The bond quality appears to be directly related to the degree of smoothness after sanding.

A step-by step procedure of the sandblasting process using the new stencil material is outlined in Illus. 10-12–10-19. This procedure is highly recommended for blasting raw wood (but with your own pretesting). For blasting pre-painted, prevarnished, or pre-lacquered surfaces it is foolish not to test first. If the results appear questionable, use the conventional stencils and supplemental adhesives.

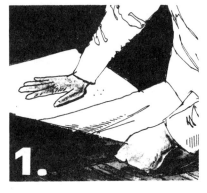

Illus. 10-12—10-15. Step 1: Place the Signblast Tape (cut slightly oversize) over the natural untreated wooden panel with the orange liner next to the wood. Strip the liner away as you pull, and apply the tape. Step 2: After the surface is completely covered with the Signblast Tape, burnish overall with a roller to remove wrinkles and to create an even bond. Step 3 (lower left): Trim excess stencil from the edges with a sharp knife or razor. Step 4: Transfer your design, with carbon paper, to the surface of the stencil. (See Illus. 10-16—10-19.)

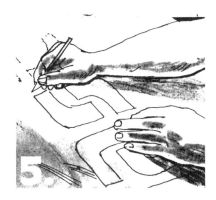

Illus. 10-16—10-19. Step 5: Cut the stencil as usual from your transferred design. Step 6: Strip away the pattern, leaving the stencil applied only to the areas that are not to be blasted away. Step 7: Blast to the depth desired to create a rich-looking carving. Step 8: When blasting is completed, remove the stencil tape. If staining or spray painting of the blasted area is to be done, leave the tape on as a masking during this process, removing it later.

Adhering the Stencil to the Wood

To blast successfully, make sure that the stencil does not come loose or lift up during blasting. Vinyl stencils can be applied with water adhesives. The easiest procedure is to completely finish the face of the sign (Illus. 10-20) with a suitable varnish or pigmented enamel before applying the stencil. This procedure enables you to remove the stencil and the remaining contact cement easily after blasting. However, clear surface finishes such as varnish are not good to use for exterior signs because they don't last. Thus, for exterior signs start with the raw, unfinished wood—either rough-sawn or smoothly sanded, depending upon the desired results.

Cut the stencil about an inch or so larger than the sign blank. Remember, you can butt small pieces of stencil together to cover large areas. Just be sure no gaps are left in the joints. Roll the stencil down (Illus. 10-21), applying pressure as you

Illus. 10-21. Rolling the stencil gives the necessary pressure to ensure a good bond.

Illus. 10-20. A sign blank pre-finished with clear varnish. Note the knotty, flat-cut boards glued together.

would in applying a plastic laminate material to a counter top. Puncture any small air bubbles that might appear. Signs that will have smooth, unblasted areas can be cleaned up by carefully hand-sanding to remove any cement left in the unblasted surfaces. Once the stencil is pressed down, the overhang can be left as is or trimmed back to the edges of the sign as desired. See Illus. 10-22–10-24. Transferring the pattern and layout is usually easier with the stencil trimmed to the edges.

We usually lay out our patterns on heavy paper and transfer the design to the stencil with carbon paper. The stencil layout is cut with a sharply pointed knife such as that shown in Illus. 10-25. This skill will take a little practice. You must cut completely through the stencil in one pass, but do not allow the point to cut too deeply. If you cut too deeply and go into the wood, the knife will tend to follow the grain of the wood rather than allowing you to make smooth-flowing curves. Use a plastic triangle or steel straightedge as a guide for cutting all the straight lines. Be sure that all lines have been cut. Peel the stencil off, exposing only those areas that are to be sandblasted (Illus. 10-26). *Caution:* Peel the stencil very carefully and pull at low angle *with* the grain. (Illus. 10-27) so that the stencil doesn't pull up large slivers of wood. After the cutting is completed and all of the stencil removed, press the stencil down with the roller once more to make sure all areas are bonded well.

When only part of a sign is to be blasted, there is no point to covering the entire sign face with the rubber stencil, which is expensive. Old pieces of

126

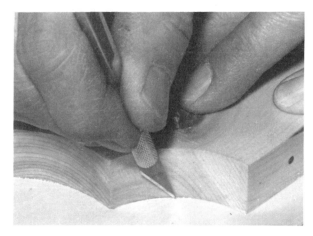

Illus. 10-22. Trimming off the excess stencil. Here the sign is pressed down against several layers of newspaper as the excess stencil is cut away.

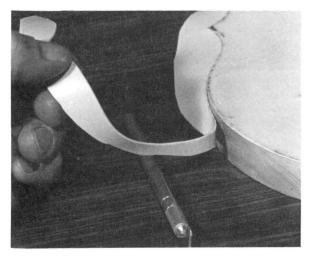

Illus. 10-23. The excess stencil is removed from the contoured edges of the sign blank prior to layout and blasting.

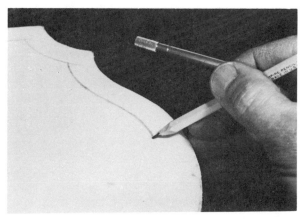

Illus. 10-24. A line for a border is finger-gauged along the contoured edge.

Illus. 10-25. Cutting the stencil. The knife is held vertically so no undercuts are made.

plywood or hardboard can be used as a protective sheathing overlapping the rubber stencil (Illus. 10-28).

Blasting a Sign

Load your blaster (Illus. 10-29), screening the abrasive into the pot. Turn on the compressor. Set your pressure to match the nozzle size. Prop your sign blank up so you can blast in a comfortable standing position. I use an old sawhorse (Illus. 10-28) for a blasting bench. Put on your safety gear (Illus. 10-30) and turn on the air at the sandblaster. With blasters having a mixture control, gradually discharge the sand from the nozzle. It is important to have the right sand adjustment. This has been achieved when a blue-colored-flamelike blast emits from the nozzle. Excessive sand retards cutting efficiency, and too little sand wastes time, energy, and air.

Illus. 10-26. The stencil has been partially removed, exposing wood areas for blasting. This job will be blasted to two levels of depth. The exposed area will be blasted first. The trees will be unmasked later and blasted to a shallower depth.

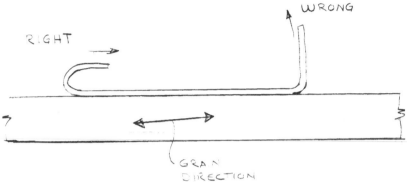

Illus. 10-27. Use a peeling motion, in a direction that is with the grain, to remove the stencil.

Illus. 10-28. Here the stencil is cut and ready for blasting. Only about one-third of the area of this sign is to be blasted, so scrap pieces of hardboard or plywood were used to make a protective sheathing over the areas not covered with the rubber stencil.

Illus. 10-29. Loading the pot and screening silica sand.

Illus. 10-30. Getting ready to blast. A lever starts and stops the abrasive stream. Note the protective helmet.

The best results will be achieved by holding the nozzle at a right angle to the work and about 6 to 12 inches away. Move the nozzle in a continuous, small circular motion over the entire surface until the desired depth is achieved. Cut to at least ½ inch in depth, somewhat less on smaller signs (Il-

lus. 10-31). If the heat generated at the blast area appears to burn the stencil material, drop the air pressure. Keep experimenting until you have the right combination of air pressure adjustment, nozzle size, sand flow efficiency, and optimum cutting time.

Once you have completed the blasting to your satisfaction, don't be too eager to remove the stencil. You may want to stain the background at this point or spray it with an aerosol, using the stencil as your paint masking. When you do remove the rubber stencil, lift it carefully, pulling at a low angle with the grain (Illus. 10-27).

One of the disadvantages of the sandblasting process is that the stencil cannot be reused once it has been removed. This is usually of minor concern because the end results are so overwhelmingly satisfactory. However, we have made reusable pre-cut letters and numbers (Illus. 10-32) with moderate success. Simply find a thin, rigid, easily cut material such as sheet polystyrene. Apply the stencil to one surface and cut the rubber and the plastic simultaneously with a shears or scroll saw. Test various contact cements until you find one that provides a suitable bond that will hold up throughout the blast (Illus. 10-33).

Some examples of easy-to-execute name signs are shown in Illus. 10-34—10-36. Illus. 10-37 shows a sign sandblasted with fine detail. Two examples of large commercial signs are presented in Illus. 10-38 and 10-39.

Illus. 10-31. The first step completed for blasting to two depths. Now the stencil will be removed from around the letters, and the trees will be blasted—but they will still be raised above the background area.

Illus. 10-32 (above left). These reusable pre-cut stencils were made by applying regular sandblast stencils onto polystyrene plastic. Illus. 10-33 (above right). This house number was sandblasted with reusable stencils.

Illus. 10-34—10-36. Some examples of small, sandblasted name signs.

Illus. 10-35.

Illus. 10-36.

Illus. 10-37. This sign shows the fine detail that can be achieved by sandblasting.

Illus. 10-38 and 10-39 (below). Large sandblasted signs. Sign at bottom has a built-up frame for extra depth. (Both signs designed and crafted by Jason Morgan.)

Illus. 10-39.

11

Finishing Signs

Woodworkers who get involved in making wood signs are usually experienced in all areas of wood-crafting and already have a good background of knowledge about wood finishing. There are a great many good reference books available that cover every aspect of wood finishing. This chapter will include only a few suggested techniques and some philosophical ideas for your consideration. Finishing wood signs is not particularly different from finishing other wood products specifically for indoor or outdoor use.

The primary reasons for finishing your sign include: (1) to improve its beauty or appearance, (2) to improve its legibility, (3) to protect it from dirt or stain, and (4) to slow down deterioration caused by weathering. With these points in mind, determine if you really want to finish the sign at all. Sometimes, in certain settings, because of the depth and shadows cast on deeply cut dimensional signs, they have just the right subtle contrast to make the sign readable but not shocking. Signs left unfinished must truly rely on the "raw" emphasis of their natural wood features (Illus. 11-1).

However, most people expect a finish on their sign because they are accustomed to having their wood products finished. Since wood is a natural, organic material it seems somewhat hypocritical to cover its best inherent features with pigmented finishes—particularly paint. Paint, in addition to its preservative qualities, is intended to cover or hide wood. It's our opinion that, whenever possible, the natural qualities of wood should be em-phasized, not hidden. If the sign must be finished, use clear, natural, non-pigment, non-glossy finishes for indoor signs. Essentially the same is recommended for outdoor signs, but the problems associated with moisture and the sun's rays must be contended with—either by directly challenging the eventual weathering problems or simply cooperating with them to remain in harmony with nature. (More about weathering later.)

This is not to say that one shouldn't paint a wood sign. If, in your opinion, paint improves the sign, paint it. Certainly paint (or any pigmented finish) adds color and emphasis, increases interest, and draws attention. Paints can be used selectively to complement the natural features of wood rather than hide them totally. When possible, select soft, "earthy" colors for backgrounds, with contrasts of

Illus. 11-1. A rustic sign is rasped to give the edge a worn, weathered look. Would finishing really make this sign look better?

darker or brighter hues for lettering and other design features needing emphasis. A wood sign that has a bright-red painted background contrasted with fluorescent yellow or gloss white is just too close to the "plastic look." A soft, light tan background, for example, with black or a dull, flat, nonglossy white lettering has good contrast, too. It's readable but not shocking or irritating—this kind of combination is more in line with the natural appearance for which wood signs are preferred in the first place. Give very careful thought and planning to your choice of finish. A perfect, artistically created sign, often involving hours of labor and tender loving care, can be ruined and cheapened quickly with just a few careless brush strokes.

Preparation

Even your most rustic types of signs should give the appearance of skill and good craftsmanship in their execution. Be sure to sand off rough fibres (hairs) that will obstruct the appearance or that will interfere with your painting or finishing work (Illus. 11-2). If the sign is to receive a clear or natural finish, be sure to remove all pencil marks that might show through the finish (Illus. 11-3). If the surfaces are intended to be smooth, then fill holes and other imperfections and follow with a careful, thorough sanding. The visibility of tool marks, dents, etc., often does more to add to the appearance of rustic signs than detract from it—it adds character and authenticity.

Illus. 11-2. Remove rough fibres with fine sandpaper.

Illus. 11-3. Remove all pencil marks. An eraser works for rough-sawn stock and sandpaper works for smooth surfaces.

Finishing Interior Signs

Indoor signs do not need protection from moisture and the sun's rays, but they generally require a higher-quality appearance and finishing. This is because the viewer is usually closer to interior signs. Almost any kind of finish can be used on indoor signs. Use penetrating Danish oils, varnishes, or lacquers for clear, natural finishes. Any of the various kinds of wood stains available today can be used to improve the color or emphasize the grain. Use exterior stains if they give you the "touch" or color you want. Most exterior stains are easier to use. Letters, borders, and artwork can be colored with any type of pigmented colors in latex, acrylics, watercolors, paints or enamels.

One idea for doing a job quickly is to use soft-tip markers to color in routed or carved letters and borders, or to color the upper surfaces of raised letters and similar surfaces, such as details of carvings. Leave the backgrounds natural. Then finish the job quickly, using a clear aerosol spray that dries fast. Thus, the job is done quickly and inexpensively without mess or cleanup.

Today, you see a lot of wooden items that are randomly burned or slightly charred with a propane or blow torch. This technique can be equally effective on wood signs—particularly the rustic types. It is a good idea to experiment on some scrap to achieve the right technique for the desired effect. Excessive charring can be removed with a bristle brush or steel wool. These burned or charred surfaces should be covered or sealed with a clear aerosol spray finish.

Illustration 11-4 shows a sign with router-cut raised letters. It was not sanded or sandblasted, nor was any liquid finish applied to it. The surfaces were thoroughly charred with a propane torch, burning away the softer areas of the wood grain and also rounding off sharply cut corners. It was then brushed vigorously with a bristle brush, like a shoe-shining brush, to remove the charred ash. Western red and white cedars, Douglas fir, spruce, and redwood work well with this technique. If this sign were left outdoors in the sun, it would eventually bleach out. For some, this might also create a very desirable effect.

Another quick technique, often employed by professionals who rout signs at fairs and amusement parks, is to use fast-drying spray paint. They spray, covering the sign completely and usually the edges as well (Illus. 11-5). After the paint dries, they remove the extra paint from the surface with a belt sander, rasp (Illus. 11-6), or hand plane (Illus. 11-7), leaving only the lettering and edges painted. Leaving about 10 percent of the paint remaining on the surface adds interest. This technique is especially effective if a rough-sawn board was used initially (Illus. 11-8). The project is usually finished with a quick-drying aerosol spray. This technique can also be employed to finish exterior signs, provided an exterior paint is used. However, it is recommended that the last step of applying the clear spray finish can be eliminated, as these finishes do not weather well at all.

Illus. 11-5. To paint routed letters quickly, use spray paint.

Illus. 11-4. This effect was achieved by thoroughly charring the sign with a propane torch.

Illus. 11-6. Clean off the surface, leaving only the painted letters.

Illus. 11-7. A hand plane, jointer, or belt sander can also be used.

Illus. 11-8. Leaving paint on some of the surface area adds a little interest.

Finishing Exterior Signs

Basically, your finishing choices are: (1) no finish at all, (2) a natural finish, (3) stains, (4) paints, or (5) a combination of any of the above. As mentioned previously, the finishing of exterior wood signs must take into account the forces of nature that tend to deteriorate wood and many finishes. The simplest approach is not to finish at all, but to cooperate with nature and allow the raw wood to weather (Illus. 11-9). This appearance is often preferred anyway since the weathered look is delightfully rustic. Some minor cracking and checking is to be expected, but other wear and tear is minimal at best. Experts say that exposed unfinished wood will wear away at a rate of only about ¼ inch every 100 years.

Illus. 11-9. This cedar sign has been left unfinished (except for the lettering) and allowed to weather naturally.

Weathering

Nearly all unfinished woods will eventually turn to a beautiful silvery grey (Illus. 11-9). Although the first color changes seem to indicate otherwise, the wood will eventually turn silver grey. The naturally colored darker woods will at first become lighter, and lighter ones will at first become darker. This is because some of the extractives (chemicals) in the wood come to the surface. But in due time the surface will turn silvery grey as it continues to be exposed to sun and moisture. According to the California Redwood Association, this change may be quickened in redwood by wetting the wood with a fine mist from a garden hose. The rate at which wood naturally reaches the optimum, weathered silvery grey will vary among different kinds of woods, and depends also upon the amount of exposure to direct sunlight and moisture. Sometimes the change may only take several months, but if the sign is facing to the north or is shaded by an overhang the total change may take a very long time, or the sign may never become uniformly weathered. For this reason, we try to avoid signs with little protective roofs over them. These roofs usually shade and protect only the upper part of the sign. The lower areas still receive sun exposure and rain. The eventual consequence is a sign face that is not uniformly weathered.

Finishing Products

Natural Exterior Finishes

At first, you might assume that a good exterior "spar" varnish is all that is required to protect your handiwork and keep its natural look well preserved under the varnish's transparent film. However, both the California Redwood Association and the Forest Products Laboratory do not recommend clear film-forming finishes, such as varnish or other synthetic resins, for long-term outdoor use. After considerable testing, they have concluded that these finishes, within a year, will turn a distasteful yellow, and will crack and peel. The only way to rectify this condition is through complete removal and total refinishing. Various penetrating oils are also not recommended for exterior finishes since they are susceptible to mildew. The two best solutions recommended for exterior finishes are water-repellent preservatives and bleaching agents.

Water-Repellent Preservatives

Water-repellent preservatives will modify the natural weathering of wood. These solutions are sold under trade names such as "Woodlife," "Pentaseal," "Wood Tox," and a number of others. These water repellents are very easy to apply and they penetrate deeply into the wood. No need to worry about lap marks, brush strokes, or runs, because they don't show. Water repellents retard the growth of fungi (mildew), keep water staining at the ends of boards to a minimum, reduce warping, and also protect woods that have a low resistance to decay. These preservative solutions can be easily applied by dipping or brushing. All edges and ends of boards should be liberally treated. Rough-sawn stock will absorb more finish than smooth surfaces, and thus the treatment will be more durable. The best application for durability and performance is achieved by repeated applications to the "point of refusal." A clear, golden tan color can be achieved on rough-sawn cedar and redwood, and the weathering problems will be greatly slowed. Eventually, however, with exposure to sun and rain, the wood will slowly turn to a driftwood grey. Water repellants also make an excellent base coat for other finishes. Consequently, the entire sign can be treated first. Then, letters and other designs, borders, etc., can be painted as desired. See Illus. 11-10. Water repellents contain toxic chemicals, so be sure to heed the warnings on the manufacturer's label.

Illus. 11-10. This sign was finished entirely with water-repellent preservative (only lettering is painted for contrast) to retard weathering.

Bleaching Oils or Stains

Bleaching oils or stains very effectively speed and advance, by chemical action, the weathered appearance. Most also contain some grey pigment that eliminates the early darkening in weathering. Bleaching solutions give an instant grey look, providing a uniform appearance during the time it takes the chemical to react with the wood and effect the color change. Bleaching produces a maintenance-free finish (Illus. 11-11). Because of the pigment, avoid leaving telltale brush-mark overlaps and runs during application. Usually only one coat is necessary because the

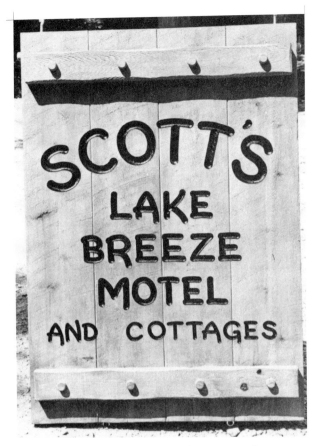

Illus. 11-11. Bleaching oils speed up natural weathering (by chemical reaction) and are one-coat, lifelong finishes.

color it produces lasts as long as the wood itself. It is not a film-forming finish and, therefore, will never blister or peel even if excessive moisture enters the wood. Inexpensively priced, bleaching solutions are available from most local paint stores and lumber dealers.

Pigmented Semi-transparent Stains

Pigmented semi-transparent stains provide color but do not hide the natural characteristics of the wood. They penetrate deeply, do not form a film on the surface of the wood, and they allow most of the grain to show through. These stains do not peel or blister, even when moisture may enter the wood. Penetrating semi-transparent stains can be used on smooth surfaces, but they will last longer on rough-sawn textured signs (Illus. 11-12). Up to 10 years' service on rough-sawn surfaces can be expected with two coats. The second coat should be applied before the first one dries, so that

Illus. 11-12. This sign background of rough-sawn cedar with semi-transparent stain has a carefree finish service-life of 10 or more years.

both coats penetrate. These stains are very easy to apply (Illus. 11-13), but care must be taken to avoid lap marks. There are many, many colors available (including some excellent natural wood tones) from your local paint dealer. Ask him for sample color "chips" to help make color selections. One company provides stains on "chips" of several different species of wood (including pine, cedar, and redwood) that are smooth on one side and rough-textured on the other.

Illus. 11-13. Applying pigmented penetrating stains to backgrounds is easy.

137

Opaque Stains

Opaque stains are more like paint because they have film-forming characteristics. These are especially good on rough-sawn backgrounds, where they last about twice as long as on smooth wood surfaces. Rough-sawn surfaces for signs are highly recommended because, even with heavily pigmented stains, more of the wood texture shows (Illus. 11-14). Opaque stains (also called solid-color stains) are preferred over paints or enamels because they are flat or dull in appearance rather than glossy. Usually only one coat is required and primers are not necessary. Opaque exterior stains are available locally.

Illus. 11-14. Opaque stain was used to finish the rough-sawn textured background of this sign.

Paints and Enamels

Paints and enamels of any serviceable exterior type can be used for coloring in letters and other details. Paints retard moisture penetration. Painted surfaces offer the best protection when achieved by this three-step procedure: (1) treat with water-repellent preservative, (2) apply primer (Illus. 11-15), and (3) apply two coats of latex, alkyd, or oil-base house paint.

Coloring Routed Lettering

Routed lettering can be colored with paints, solid-color stains, or exterior enamels and can be done

Illus. 11-15. To obtain the greatest degree of durability, prime raised letter-surfaces before painting.

by careful application with artist's brushes (Illus. 11-16). A sharp line should exist where the surface of the letter meets the background surface of the sign. Another system that shows much promise is pour-in epoxy for signs with flat-bottomed, engraved lettering. It is best applied to raw, unfinished wood. Epoxy resins suitable for exterior use do the job quickly and easily when measured, pigment is added (about 1 teaspoon per cup of resin), and they are mixed and simply poured in (Illus. 11-17). Simply pour a "bead" onto the approximate center area of each letter. The resin tends to flow out to the edges and will self-level. See Illus. 11-18 and 11-19. The sign must remain level and should be covered with some sort of dust shield until the resin cures. One disadvantage of this technique is

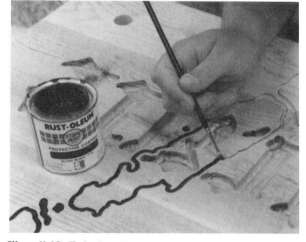

Illus. 11-16. Painting in narrow router cuts requires a steady hand.

Illus. 11-17. With the container crimped to form a pouring spout, the pigmented epoxy is poured onto the routed letter-surfaces.

Illus. 11-18. A small stick is used to spread the resin towards the uncovered areas of each letter.

Illus. 11-19. The flow-coated resin in the letters will level off to a very smooth finish and will be permanently welded to the wood.

that letters that are not cut cleanly may have an ink-blotter effect around rough fibres, in which case the resin is pulled somewhat beyond the containing edge of the letter and into the background. When you stain the background later, any excess that may drip or run onto the cured epoxy lettering can be wiped off easily with a rag.

Coloring Cutout Letters

Cutout letters are often colored with transparent or opaque, solid-color stains before they are attached to their appropriate backgrounds. See Illus. 11-20 and 11-21. Always finish all surfaces, when possible, for resistance to moisture and for balance to reduce warping tendencies.

Applying Reflective Sheeting and Paints

Reflective sheeting and paints are sometimes appropriately applied to sign lettering. Various materials in many colors are available to allow nighttime reading when viewed by reflected light. Flexible, reflective sheeting with an adhesive-coated backing makes application easy onto most clean, dry, and smooth surfaces. It generally has a life range of five to six years. Liquid reflective coatings, available in a limited number of colors, are applied like paint and last from four to seven years without recoating. The paint-on coatings are unobtrusive during daytime viewing, as they have a textured satin finish. Materials of this type are available at paint and household hardware stores locally.

Preservative Treatment for Posts

Preservative treatment for posts (Illus. 11-22), when necessary, should be done at the most opportune time—preferably before other finishes have been applied to the in-ground areas of the post. Several coats are best and these can often be applied simultaneously with other finish coats. Give the posts a heavy, generous coat just prior to installation. Refer to page 11 for information about post materials that do not need any brush-on preservatives.

Illus. 11-20. Cutout letters finished with transparent stain. Highlighted routed edges are solid-color.

Illus. 11-21. A painted letter, with the routed edge highlighted for interest and contrast.

Illus. 11-22. These posts are getting the last coat of preservative just before they are set into the ground.

12

Guidelines for Starting a Wood-Sign Business

Pricing

Those who are starting a wood-sign business are probably wondering what to charge for a sign. It is difficult to recommend specific prices. Everyone has different expenses in tools, materials, types of job orders, etc. Individuals also have different levels of skill and efficiency in their work. Furthermore, wages and other costs constantly change in this whirlwind economy.

Only you know (or can determine) what your actual costs are. Only you can determine what wage or salary you must have. Only you can determine what profit margin is necessary for reinvestment into your business.

If your real intent is to make a viable business out of this craft, seek some general business counseling. Get the advice of your banker and visit an accountant or bookkeeper for help and assistance with your record keeping. You will need to calculate all of your overhead costs. This involves much more than just wood, glue, and paint. Your overhead includes such things as monthly rent or mortgage payments, taxes, insurance, and all utilities (including phone, electric, heat, and water). Tools, equipment, building depreciation, travel, hired help, and other supplies such as pencils, postage, stock material, etc., all must be included on your list of expenses.

Convert all your yearly and monthly expenses to weekly, and then reduce them to an hourly expense figure. This is your overhead and your fixed cost. To this, add your own hourly wage plus the cost of the materials (include waste) involved in each job. To this, add a percentage for profit. Profit can range from 20 to 100%. Profit is necessary because it provides the funding for the growth and expansion of your business. To do all of this requires much paperwork and record keeping. Obviously, you must keep track of how long it takes to lay out, carve, rout, or blast signs. From all this data, you can then calculate a fair price based upon square or linear sign footage.

In general, it is recommended that you charge 35 to 40% more for engraved routed letter work than single-stroke routed letters. On double-faced signs, both routed and sandblasted, charge 50 to 70% above the price of a single-faced sign, depending upon the material and detail involved.

As far as pricing is concerned, refer to *The Signwriter's Guide to Easier Pricing*, a reference book that deals with the average rates within the entire sign industry. This is an expensive little booklet that is updated frequently. It gives current hourly rates for all aspects of sign work. For example, it specifies the suggested hourly trade rates for all phases of artwork, painting, and sign installation, along with specific pricing data for routed and sandblasted signs of all sizes. A section is also devoted to charges for cutout letters in different heights and materials. This valuable little booklet has been the blue book of the sign industry for almost a decade. It can be ordered from *Signs of the Times* and *Sign Craft* magazines. See page 143 for the addresses.

If you do a lot of repetitive small residential name signs you can make up an illustrated price list and order form, as shown in Illus. 12-2. Simply lay out the sample shapes and list any options and special charges that are relative to your own operation. Once this is done, have the original reproduced by photocopy or instant printing. With carbon paper you can give your customer a copy and keep one copy for your work orders and income records. Above all, it is very important to keep track of all of your costs, both for establishing your own pricing and for your tax deductions.

You will not make it by accepting less than a fair price just to get a job or to undercut a competitor. Don't worry about the wood sign maker down the road who charges less. He will soon tire of working for nothing (as would you) and eventually close his operation. Keep your prices at least comparable to those of the skilled tradespeople in your area. If you are conscientious and put out quality signs, you will not have to worry. You will get repeat business from satisfied customers. Having signs representative of your best efforts out there in the public's eye is your best advertising.

Doing the larger signs presents more risks, especially if you do not price them right. Clients who intend to order a large sign want to know their cost before you start. Avoid quick verbal prices unless you are certain. We have found that it is good business to give prices for larger signs in writing (that is, as a written quotation).

Pricing begins with a consultation with the prospective customer to establish what he actually wants. Then, when you're alone, take the time to slowly think through the job. Do your calculations and double-check—you do not want to miss anything. Put your quotation in the form of a letter and mail it to the prospect.

Some specifications to include in your quotation are the overall size, one or two sides, kind of materials, how assembled, style and size of letters, if and how finished and if delivery, installation (any electrical), and whether or not local taxes are included. It is also a good idea to develop a standard statement of disclaimer with regard to certain liabilities, such as zoning ordinances, installation, service life, etc. This makes it clear to the customer that he assumes all such relevant liabilities. Another important subject to spell out very clearly in your quotation letter is the financial terms. It is not unreasonable to ask for an advance of 50% with the order and the balance to be paid on completion. Avoid extending credit. Finally, it is only fair to the customer to state the time you will need to complete the job, such as "3 to 4 weeks to completion."

Subcontracting

Remember that your ultimate objective is to put out only good signs and to do them as financially equitably as possible for yourself and your client. Rather than risk your reputation by doing a job, or part of a job, that just doesn't measure up, explore the possibility of subcontracting. That is, simply hire someone to do the work for you that you are not equipped to handle yourself. If you have problems with layout, hire an artist, designer, or sign painter. If you are not equipped to prepare and glue-up large panels, go to a cabinet shop. There certainly isn't anything wrong with going to another sign shop to hire airbrush or gold-leaf work. Be sure to get a firm price beforehand so you can include it in the quotation to your client. Add 10 to 20% extra for your legwork, time, and paperwork. It is almost impossible to be all-skilled and all-efficient in all areas of a wood sign business. One day you will get a request for a routed sign with raised gold-leaf letters, the next day it is a sandblasted job with airbrush, etc.

NAME:_____

ADDRESS: _____

_____

PHONE: _____ PICK-UP:_____

SMALL SIGNS: (W/BLACK SPRAY PAINT)
(SMOOTH SURFACE)

A. [rectangle] SMALL
(1" x 4" x 16")

B. [wavy-edge sign] MEDIUM
(1" x 6" x 18")

C. [ornate rectangle sign] LARGE
(1" x 8" x 20")

ADD # FOR SHAPES B & C

SHAPE	SIZE	1-SIDE	2-SIDES
	SMALL	#	#
	MEDIUM	#	#
	LARGE	#	#

ADDITIONAL CHARGE FOR MORE THAN ONE LINE.
ADDITIONAL CHARGE FOR LARGER SIGNS.
ALL PRICES PLUS   % TAX

Illus. 12-1. A simplified version of a combination order form and price list for standardized name signs.

Trade Publications

In order to keep abreast of what is going on in the sign trade around the country, you will want authoritative, current information. There are two excellent publications well worth examining. One is *Signs of the Times*, a monthly magazine available from Signs of the Times Publishing Co., 407 Gilbert Ave., Cincinnati, OH 45202. The other is a fairly new quarterly publication called *Sign Craft*, available from Sign Craft, 1938 Hill Ave., Fort Myers, FL 33906. Both magazines allot plenty of space to wood signs, contain relevant how-to articles, and are valuable sources for locating special supplies. They also sponsor sign design awards, give association notices, and often publish a cost or pricing analysis for wood signs.

13

Keeping Your Tools Sharp

It is of major importance to be sure to keep your tools extremely sharp. This cannot be overly stressed. Trying to work with dull tools will discourage a novice faster than anything else. Dull tools will tear or crush the fibres of softwood, and will require more force or energy when used to carve hardwoods. With properly sharpened tools, both softwoods and hardwoods will carve surprisingly easily.

While making, edging, framing, and installing signs, you will use several different cutting tools. This chapter covers sharpening drills, router bits, chisels, blades, etc. Successful sharpening of cutting tools depends mostly upon the use of the correct grinding wheel, the setup or holding of the tool, and the method of grinding.

Grinding wheels available to the do-it-yourself sign-maker are of limited variety. Most wheels that come on bench grinders when you buy them are for snagging and rough grinding. They are very hard and will burn your precision hand tools and therefore destroy the cutting edges. Through Sears' catalog departments, you can purchase soft grinding wheels for sharpening tools made of high-speed steel. These new wheels will not burn and therefore will not soften your tools. When sharpening carbide, use a silicon carbide wheel. Conventional wheels made of aluminum oxide will not grind carbide. These silicon carbide wheels are generally green in color and are readily available.

When you use the proper wheel, and hold the tool at the proper angle, with controlled feed and oscillation, sharpening is a simple task. On the next several pages are grinder accessories designed to hold and control tools while you are sharpening them. These accessories can be used with bench grinders and are not expensive.

Safety is your business in both the application and care of grinding wheels. Wheels improperly used may not only be breakable—they can be dangerous. Read and apply the rules for safe operation in the owner's manual of your grinder and on the wheels themselves.

The Sears model 6672 Drill Bit Sharpener, shown in Illus. 13-2, is available at Sears stores or from Sears catalog departments. Collets hold the drill on center to ensure that the point is sharpened accurately on center. Grinding is done on the front face of the wheel. Sharpening is accomplished by turning the barrel and feeding in a fine-feed screw. Lip clearance is controlled by a cam that feeds the drill in as you turn the barrel. Using the proper grinding wheel will help in getting the proper results without burning. When an accurate hole is required in wood, such as for dowelling, a wood point is helpful. By dressing a small corner chamfer on the grinding wheel and using the Drill Bit Sharpener, a wood point can be ground (Illus. 13-3).

While carving wood signs, chisels and other straight blades will need to be sharpened. The Tool Holder Attachment (Illus. 13-5) will hold the tool to be sharpened at the correct angle. A rack-

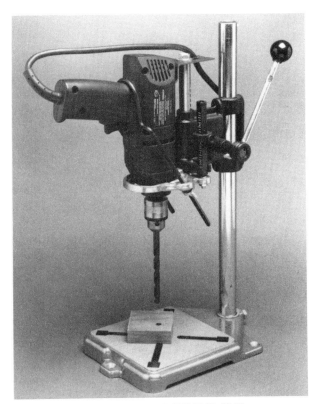

Illus. 13-1. The Sears model 25921 Drill Press Stand can be used to convert any Craftsman ¼- or ⅜-inch electric hand drill into a drill press. This will ensure easy, accurate drilling.

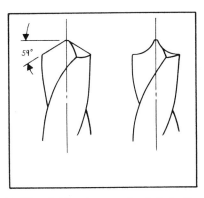

Illus. 13-3. The drill point on the left is the conventional 59-degree point that comes on most drills. The bit on the right is ground for drilling accurately in wood.

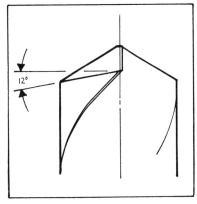

Illus. 13-4. Lip clearance is necessary for a drill to cut freely. The Sears model 6672 Drill Bit Sharpener gives equal clearance to both lips.

Illus. 13-2. The Sears model 6672 Drill Bit Sharpener is used with bench grinders.

Illus. 13-5. The Sears Tool Holder Attachment will hold chisels and plane blades at the correct angle. It will control the oscillation and infeed and can be used with any bench grinder. It is available at Sears catalog and retail outlets.

and-pinion feed gives an even cross-feed and there is a fine adjusting screw for infeed. Use a fine-grit hand stone to deburr the cutting edge. Chisels can be sharpened really well with this product.

Most chisels are sharpened at 60 degrees; just sharpen them at the same angle as when purchased. Grind only a little at a time until sharp. Chisels are made of tempered steel and can be softened if they are overheated.

A dressing stick (Illus. 13-6) can also be clamped in the tool holder for trueing and cleaning grinding wheels. Dressing is necessary to keep the wheel straight across the face and to clean the wheel if it becomes loaded. This dressing stick has a silicone carbide stone that is harder than the grinding wheels. Therefore, it will cut away the surface.

Illus. 13-6. The Sears model 6491 Grinding Wheel Dressing Stick is also available at Sears retail and catalog stores. Use it with the Tool Holder (shown in Illus. 13-5) for best results.

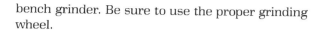
bench grinder. Be sure to use the proper grinding wheel.

Illus. 13-8. The Sears model 6660 Router Bit Sharpener is used to sharpen high-speed steel router bits that have a ¼-inch shank.

Always sharpen the router bit on the front face, not on the outer edge or outside diameter. Grinding on the outer edge will alter the shape of the bit and it will no longer cut the same shape groove.

The Sears Router Bit Sharpener can be adjusted so that each bit's cutting edge comes in contact

GRINDING WHEEL

Illus. 13-7. Sharpen the router bit on the front of its cutting edge so as not to change its size or shape.

Keep your router bits sharp and clean for smooth and easy cutting. Use gum and pitch remover as needed to keep them clean. Use the Sears Router Bit Sharpener (Illus. 13-7) to keep them sharp. This attachment can be used with any

Illus. 13-9. The Sears model 21645 Tool Grinding and Sharpening Handbook contains information on tool sharpening. It is useful for anyone who makes wood signs.

with the grinding wheel at the proper angle. A detent ensures that both lips are ground the same.

These many bench grinder accessories make your bench grinder a sharpening machine. The products described in this chapter are listed in Sears' *Power and Hand Tool Catalog*. A free copy of the *Power and Hand Tool Catalog* is available from Sears catalog departments.

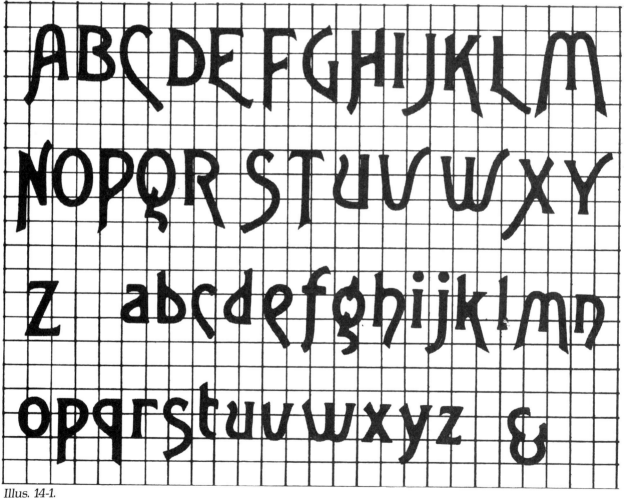

14

Patterns and Design Ideas

Following are a wide variety of letter and number patterns that can be used to make wood signs.

Illus. 14-1.

Illus. 14-2.

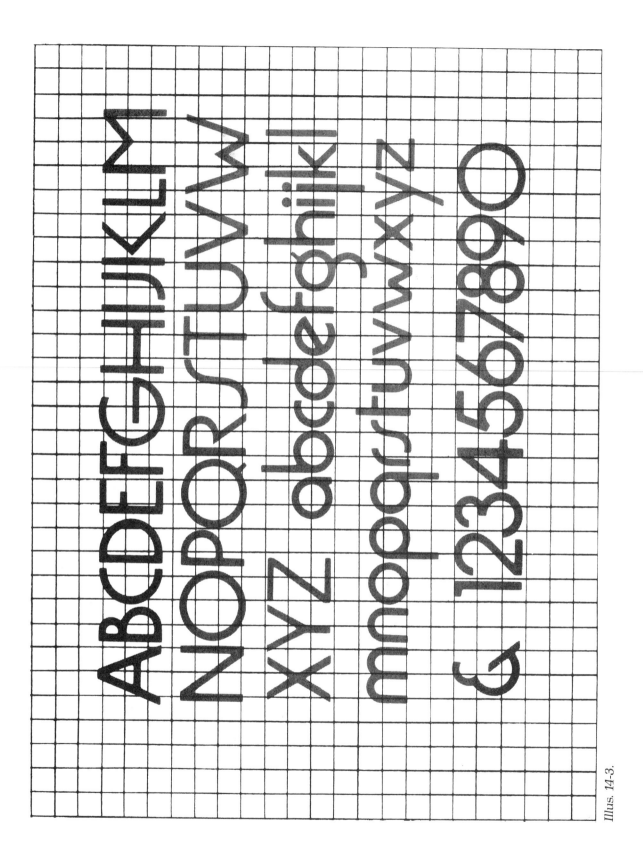

ABCDEFGHIJKLM
NOPQRSTUVW
XYZ abcdefghijkl
mnopqrstuvwxyz
& 1234567890

Illus. 14-3.

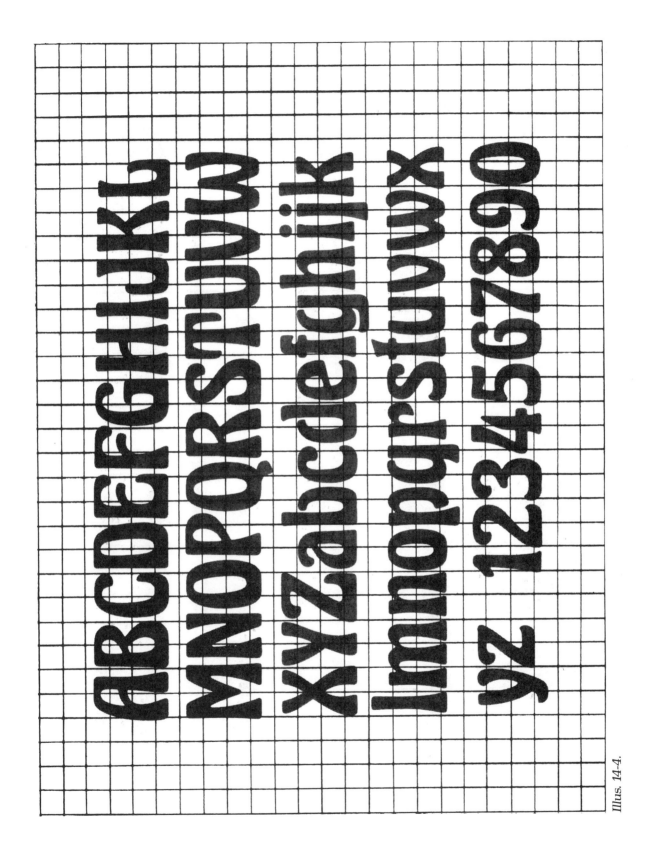

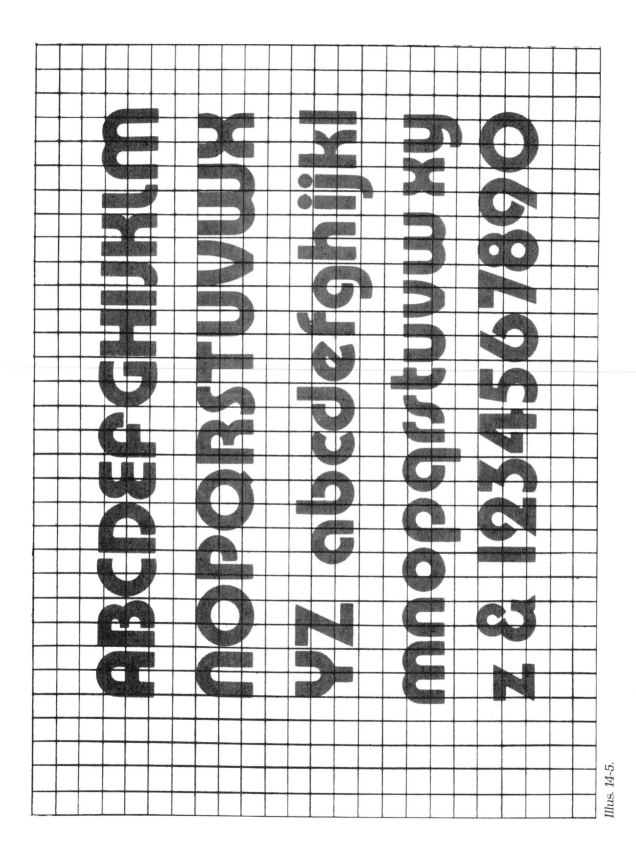

ABCDEFGHIJKLM
NOPQRSTUVWX
YZ abcdefghijkl
mnopqrstuvwxy
z & 1234567890

Illus. 14-5.

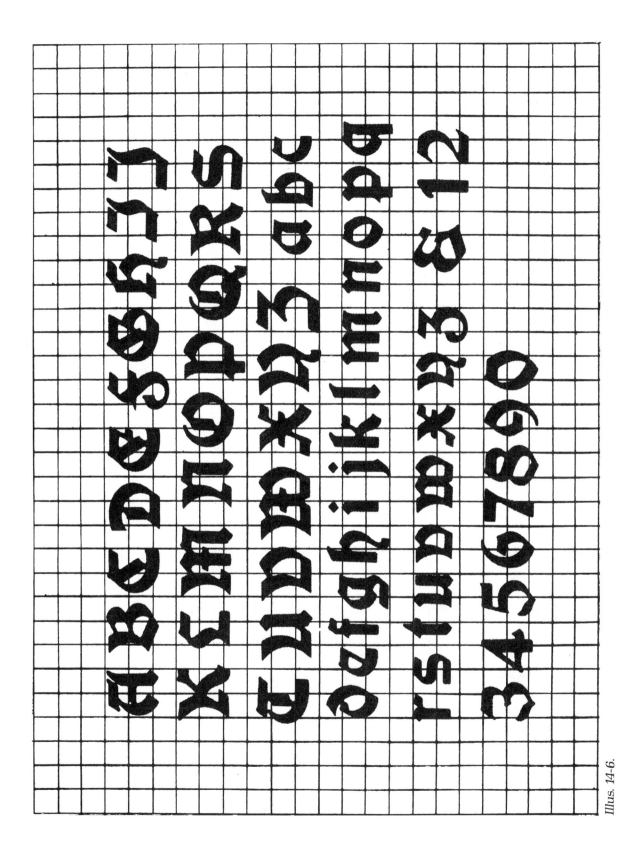

Illus. 14-6.

153

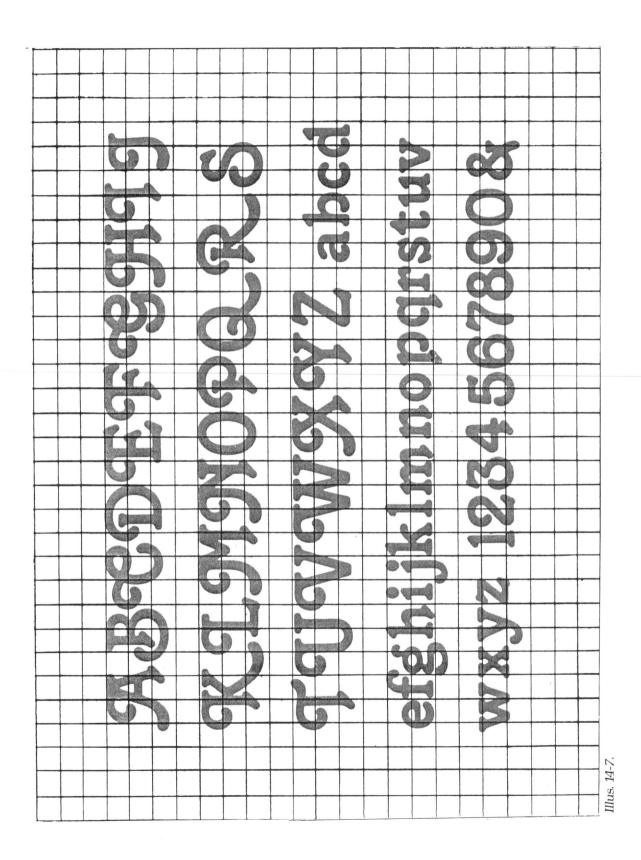

Illus. 14-7.

154

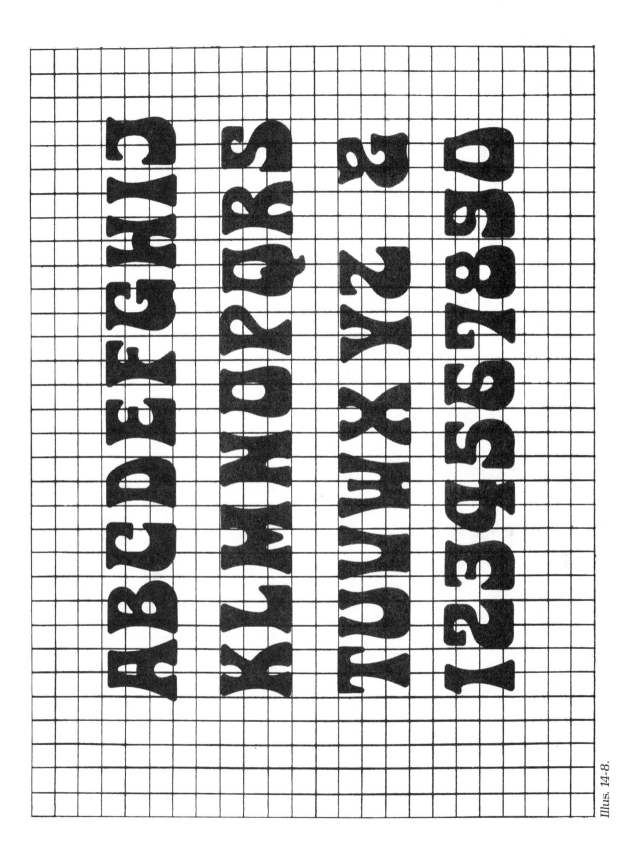

ABCDEFGHIJ
KLMNOPQRS
TUVWXYZ
1234567890

Illus. 14-8.

155

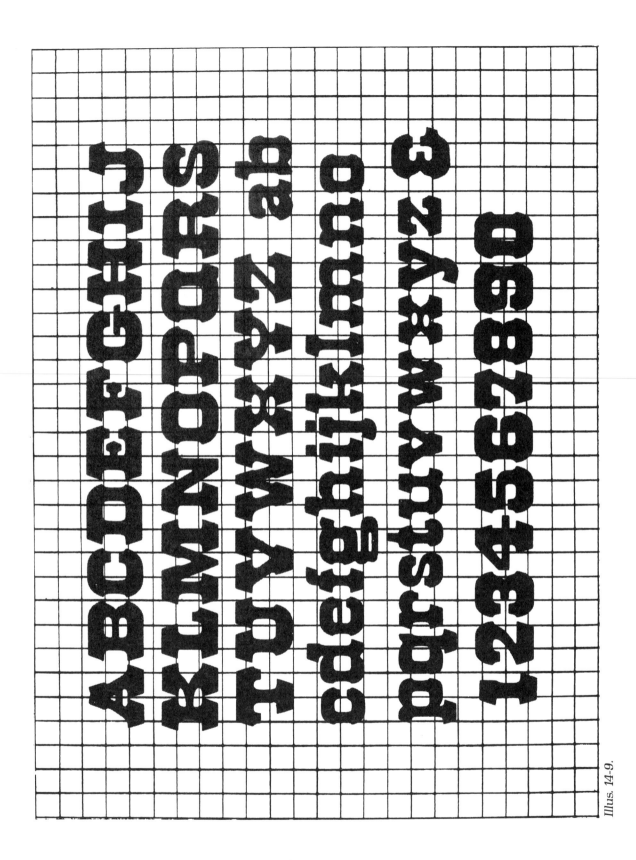

ABCDEFGHIJ
KLMNOPQRS
TUVWXYZ ab
cdefghijklmno
pqrstuvwxyz
1234567890

Illus. 14-9.

156

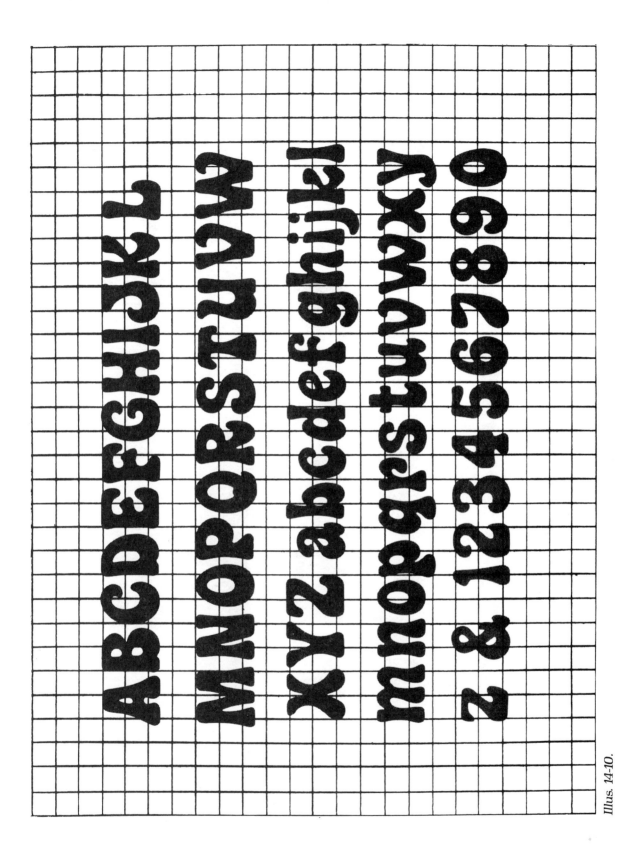

ABCDEFGHIJKL
MNOPQRSTUVW
XYZ abcdefghijel
mnopqrstuvwxy
z & 1234567890

Illus. 14-10.

157

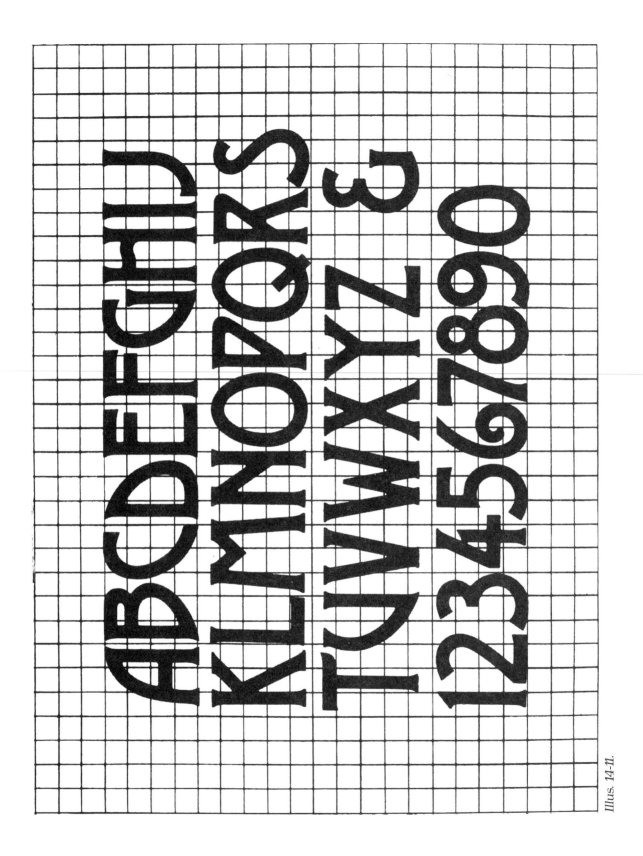

ABCDEFGHIJ
KLMNOPQRS
TUVWXYZ
1234567890

Illus. 14-11.

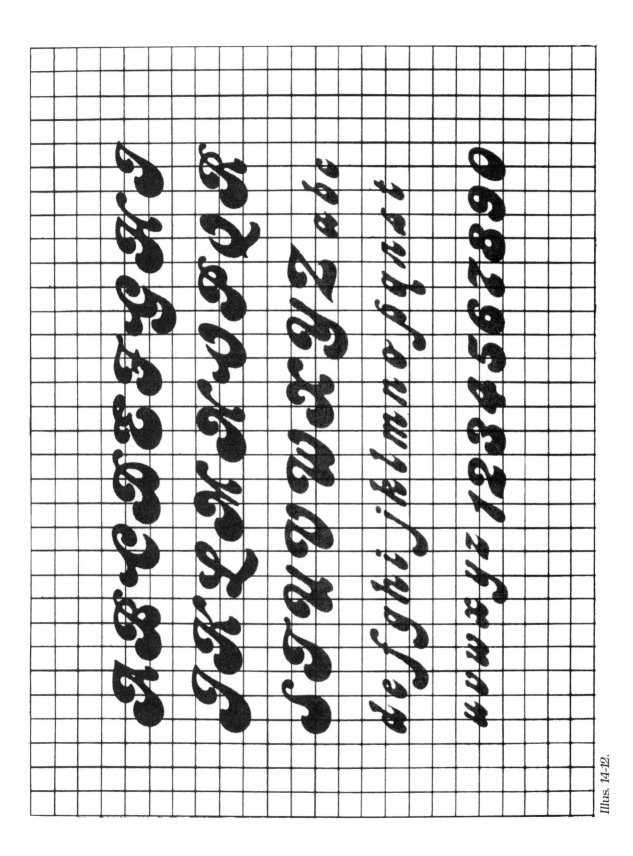

Illus. 14-12.

Illus. 14-13—14-18. Patterns for Gay Nineties uppercase letters and numbers.

Illus. 14-14.

Illus. 14-15.

Illus. 14-16.

Illus. 14-17.

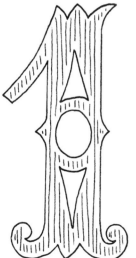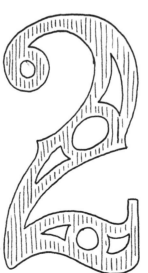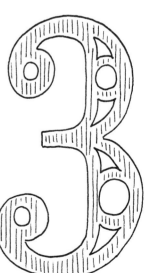

164

Illus. 14-18.

165

Illus. 14-19.

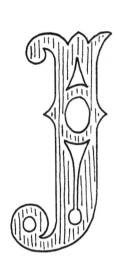
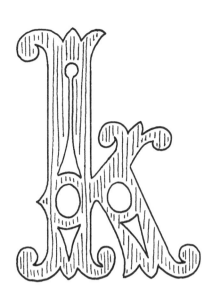
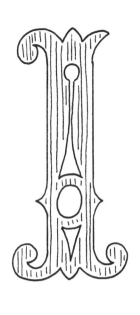

Illus. 14-20.

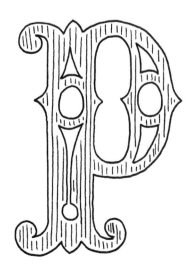

Illus. 14-21.

Illus. 14-22.

Illus. 14-23.

170

Illus. 14-24.

Illus. 14-25.

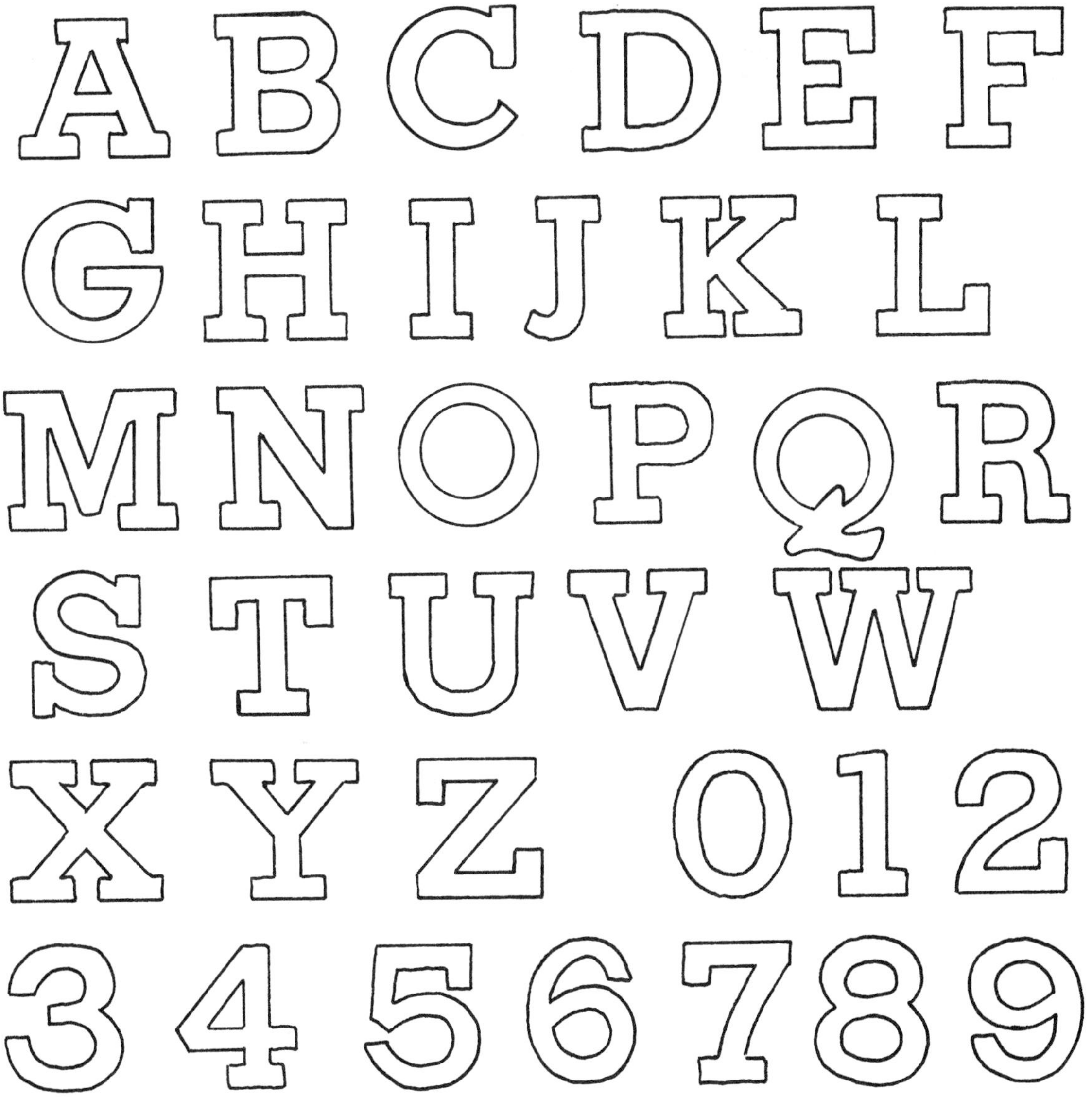

ABCDEF
GHIJKL
MNOPQR
STUVW
XYZ 012
3456789

Illus. 14-26.

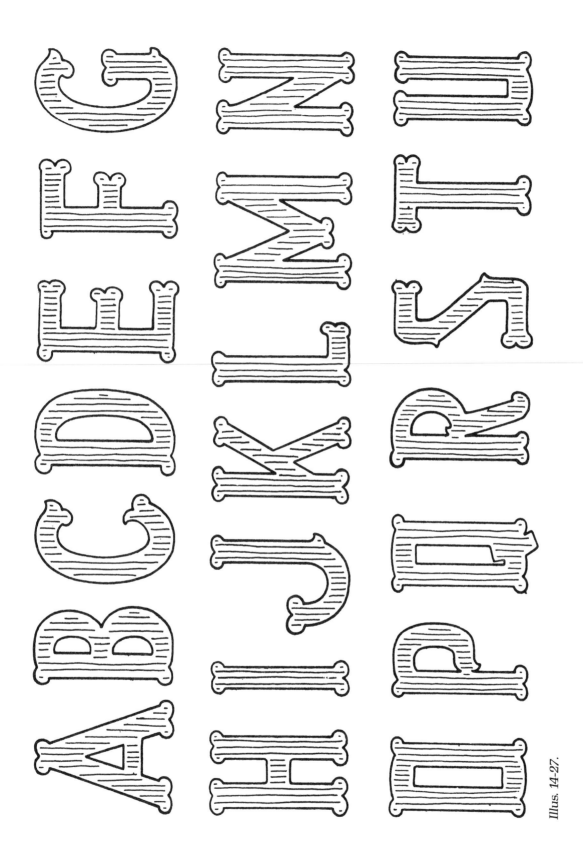

Illus. 14-27.

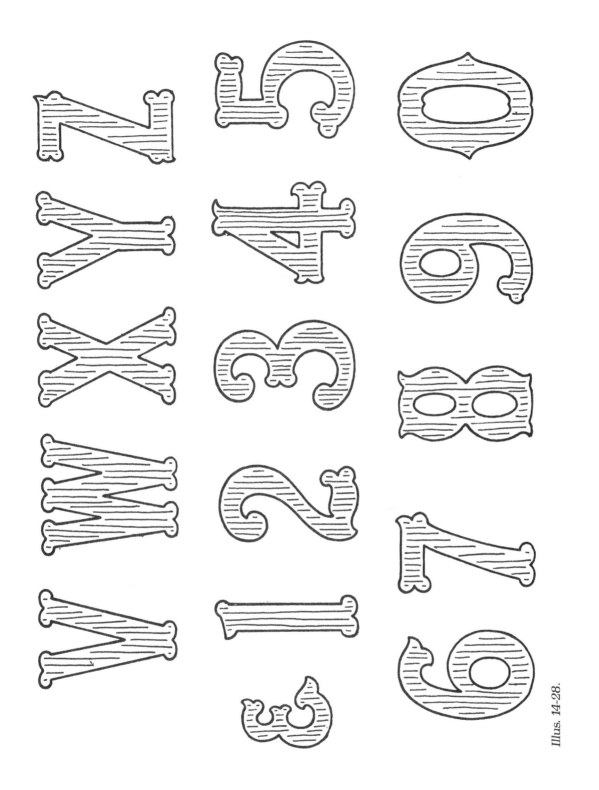

Illus. 14-28.

Illus. 14-29—14-34. Country patterns.

Illus. 14-30.

Illus. 14-31.

Illus. 14-32.

179

Illus. 14-33.

Illus. 14-34.

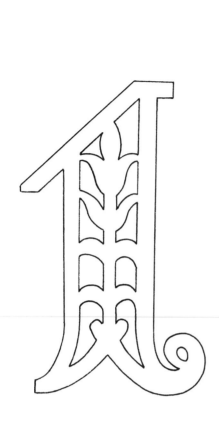

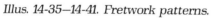

Illus. 14-35—14-41. Fretwork patterns.

Illus. 14-36.

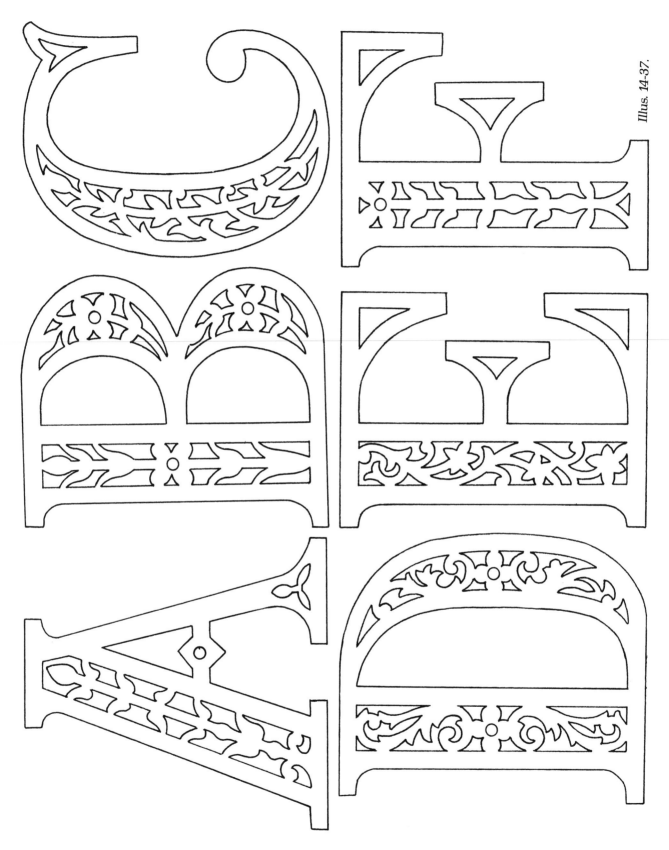

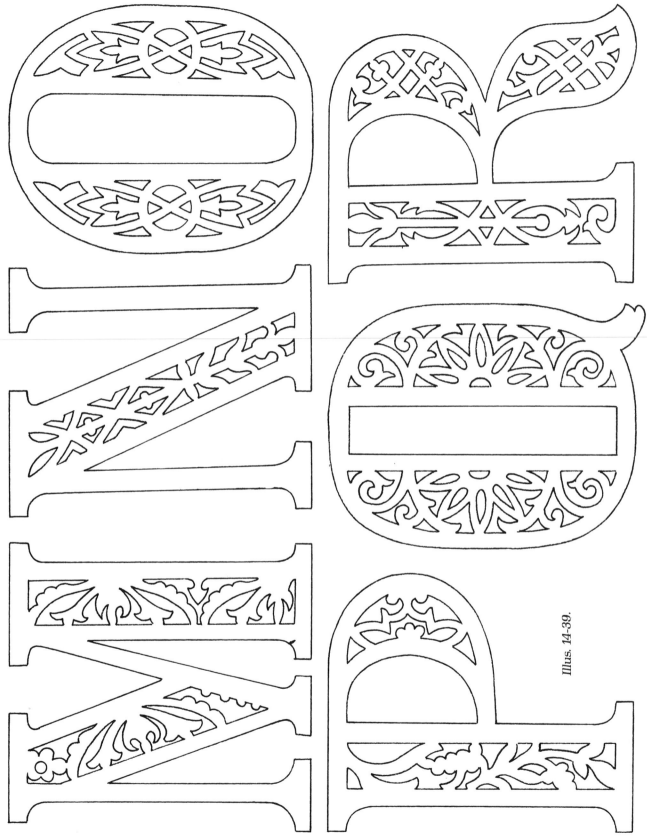

Illus. 14-39.

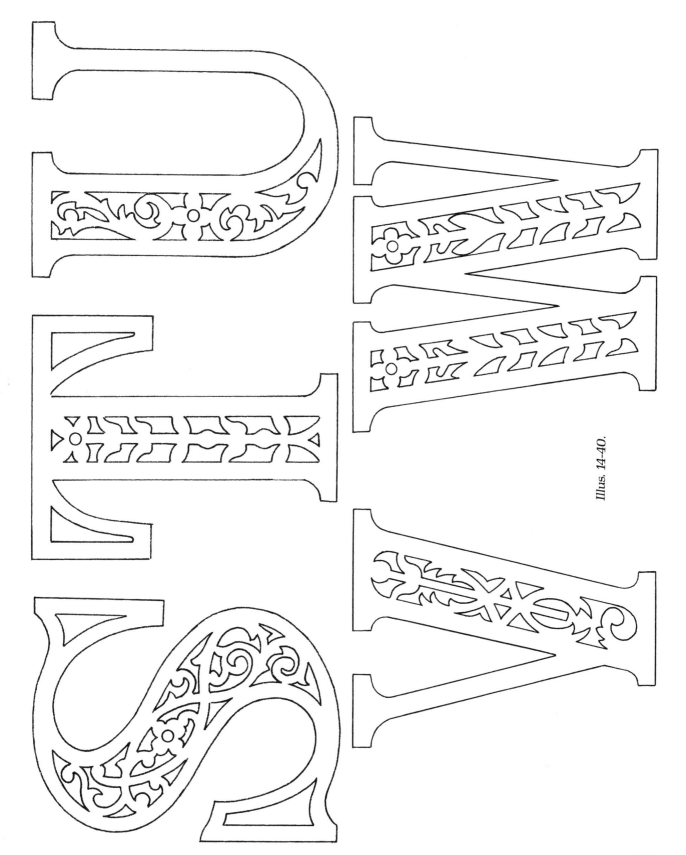

Illus. 14-40.

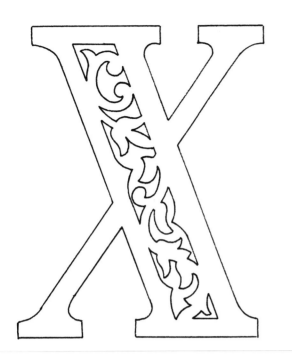

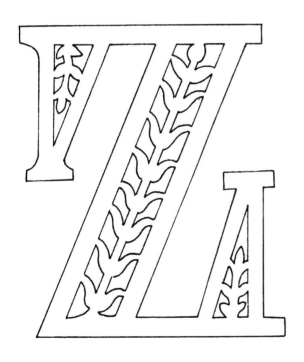

Illus. 14-41.

188

Illus. 14-42 and 14-43. Victorian patterns.

Illus. 14-43.

Color Section
Photo Credits

Page *C*: Luckley House sign by William J. Schnute, Oak Leaves Studio. Page D: The Rushes sign by Wayne Detjen, Wood Graphics Div., Wis. Label Corp.

Index

Air compressors, 122
Alphabet patterns, 47–48, 52–53,
  84, 86, 148–190
Carving, 61
  of incised letters, 61–63
  of raised letters, 64–65
  of round forms in relief, 66–67
Circle routing, 92
Clamps, 37–38
Cutout letters, 39, 96–97
  coloring, 139
  designs for, 45–46
  mounting, 43
  plywood, 40
  solid-wood, 40–43
  standoff type, 43–45
Deluxe Pantograph (Sears model
  #25187), 97–98
Design(s)
  analysis of, 16–18
  computer-assisted, 27–33
  for cutout letters, 45–46
  letter size and, 18–19
  letter spacing and, 19
  preparing art for projection and,
    24–27
  transferring to wood, 27
  word arrangement and, 21–24
Dressing stick, 145
Drill Bit Sharpener (Sears model
  #6672), 144–147
Enamels, 138
Engraved letters, 70
Finishing
  of exterior signs, 135
  of interior signs, 133–134
  preparation for, 133
  reasons for, 132
  weathering and, 135
Finishing products, 136–139
Flat grain, vs. vertical grain, 121
Foot pedal (Sears model #25172),
  101
Freehand-routed engraving, 73–75,
  79–80
Gouges, 36
Grinding wheels, 144
Hand-carved signs, 59–60
  short-cuts, 68–69
  tools for, 60–61
Holes, drilling and boring of, 37
Huge signs, making, 115–118
Incised letters, carving of, 61–63

Interior signs
  finishing of, 133–134
  woods for, 9
Large signs, 102, 108–114
Letter routing, with templates, 93
Letters, cutout. See Cutout letters
Letter stencil set (Sears model
  #2518), 97
Letter template kit (Sears model
  #2573), 93
Miniature Sign Layout Kit (Sears
  model #25196), 99–100
Numerical patterns, 48, 53–54, 84,
  149–159, 164–167, 175–176,
  181–183, 190
Oil finishes, 133
Opaque projectors, 24
Opaque stains, 138
Overhead projectors, 24
Paints, 132–133, 138–139
Planing tools, 35–36
Plywood
  for cutout letters, 40
  types of, 14–15
Posts
  for large signs, 107, 110
  preservative treatment for, 139
  for Victorian sign, 56–58
Pounce wheel, 27
Relief work, 59
  carving, 64–65
  carving round forms in, 66–67
  routed signs, 70–73
Rotary Pantograph (Sears model
  #26003), 97
Rout-A-Copier (Sears model
  #25126), 100–101
Rout-A-Signer (Sears model
  #2572), 98–99
Routed signs, 70
  freehand engraving, 73–75
  projects, 75–80
  single-stroke freehand work,
    80–87
Router(s), 36, 72
Router bits, 36–37, 73, 87, 96, 97
Routing
  making square base for, 94–95
  of perfect circles, 92
Routing aids, 87–91
Safety, 4, 73, 144
Sandblasters, 121–123

Sandblasting, 119
  adhering stencil to wood,
    126–127
  equipment for, 121–127
  knots and, 121
  procedure for sign, 127–131
  woods for, 120–121
Sanders, 37–38
Sears Power and Hand Tool Catalog,
  78–147
Shaping tools, 36
Signblast Tape, 124–125
Sign Layout Kit (Sears model
  #25176), 39, 45, 95–96
Sign routing and carving
  machines, 96–101. See also
  specific machines
Stains, 136–138
Standoff letters, 43–45
Template-routing, 75–80
Tool Holder Attachment, 145
Tools, 34–38. See also specific
  tools
  for hand-carved signs, 60–61
  sharpening, 144–147
T-square guide
  for routing, 89–91
  using, to make square base,
    94–95
Upstroke, 80
Vacuum attachment, for router, 72
Victorian sign-post, 56–58
Victorian signs, 46, 49–55
  alphabet pattern, 52–53
  border for, 55
  numerical patterns, 53–54
  sign-board backer, 49–51
Weathering, 135
Wood(s)
  for exterior signs, 9–10
  for interior signs, 9
  plywoods, 14–15
  pressure-treated, 11
  requirements for sign-making, 9
  for sandblasting, 120–121
  selecting and buying lumber,
    11–12
  transferring pattern to, 27
Wood-sign business
  potential for, 7
  pricing, 141–142
  subcontracting, 142
  trade publications for, 143